CANADA IN FLANDERS (VOLUME III)

LECTOR HOUSE PUBLIC DOMAIN WORKS

CANADA IN FLANDERS
(VOLUME III)

CHARLES G. D. ROBERTS,
MAX AITKEN BEAVERBROOK

9 789356 146099
ISBN: 978-93-5614-609-9

Published: 1918

LECTOR HOUSE

LECTOR HOUSE LLP
E-MAIL: info@lectorhouse.com

CANADA IN FLANDERS (VOLUME III)

THE OFFICIAL STORY OF THE CANADIAN EXPEDITIONARY FORCE

BY

MAJOR CHARLES G. D. ROBERTS

WITH A PREFACE BY
LORD BEAVERBROOK

WITH MAPS AND APPENDICES

IN THREE VOLUMES,
VOL. III.

MCMXVIII

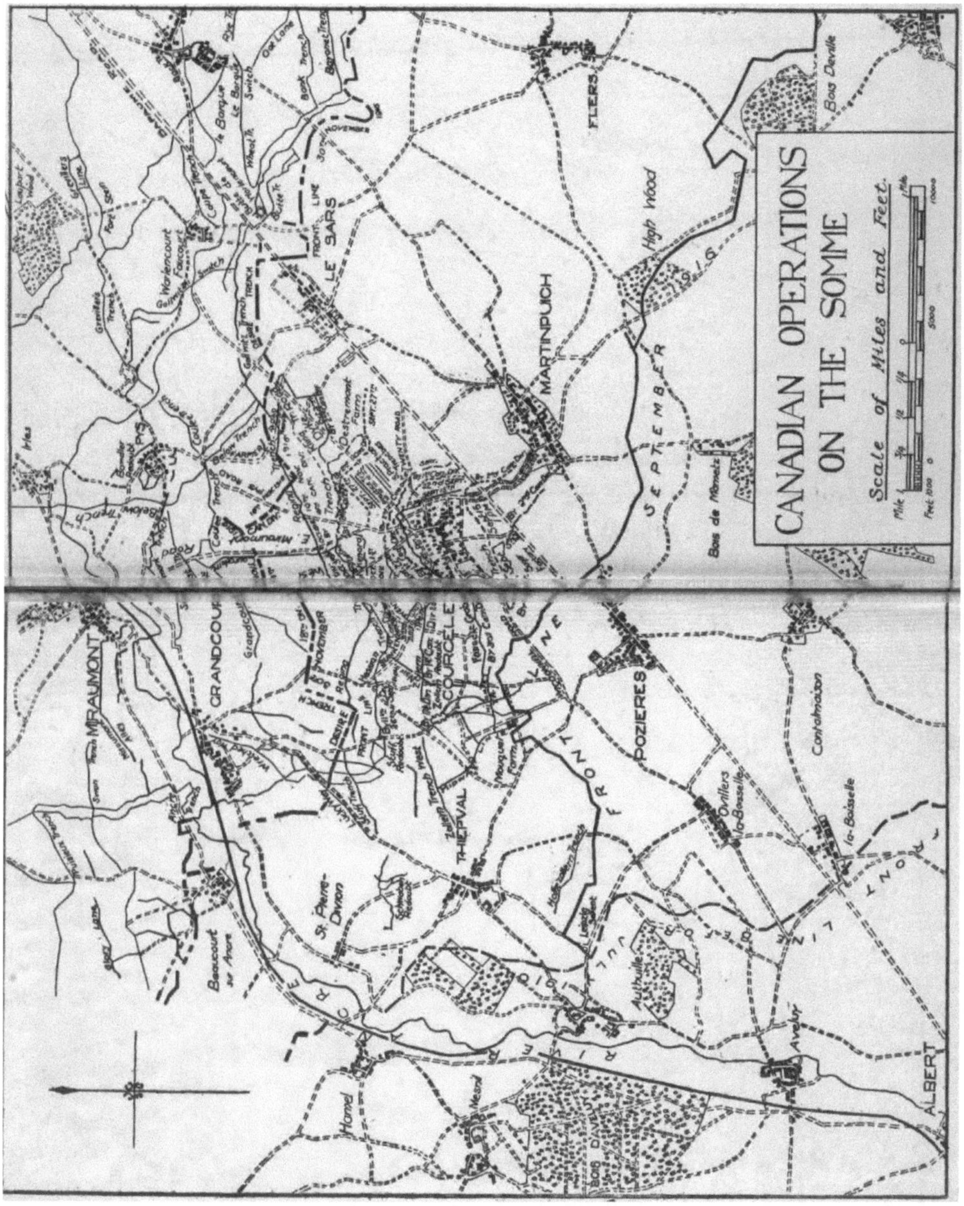

Map—Canadian Operations on the Somme

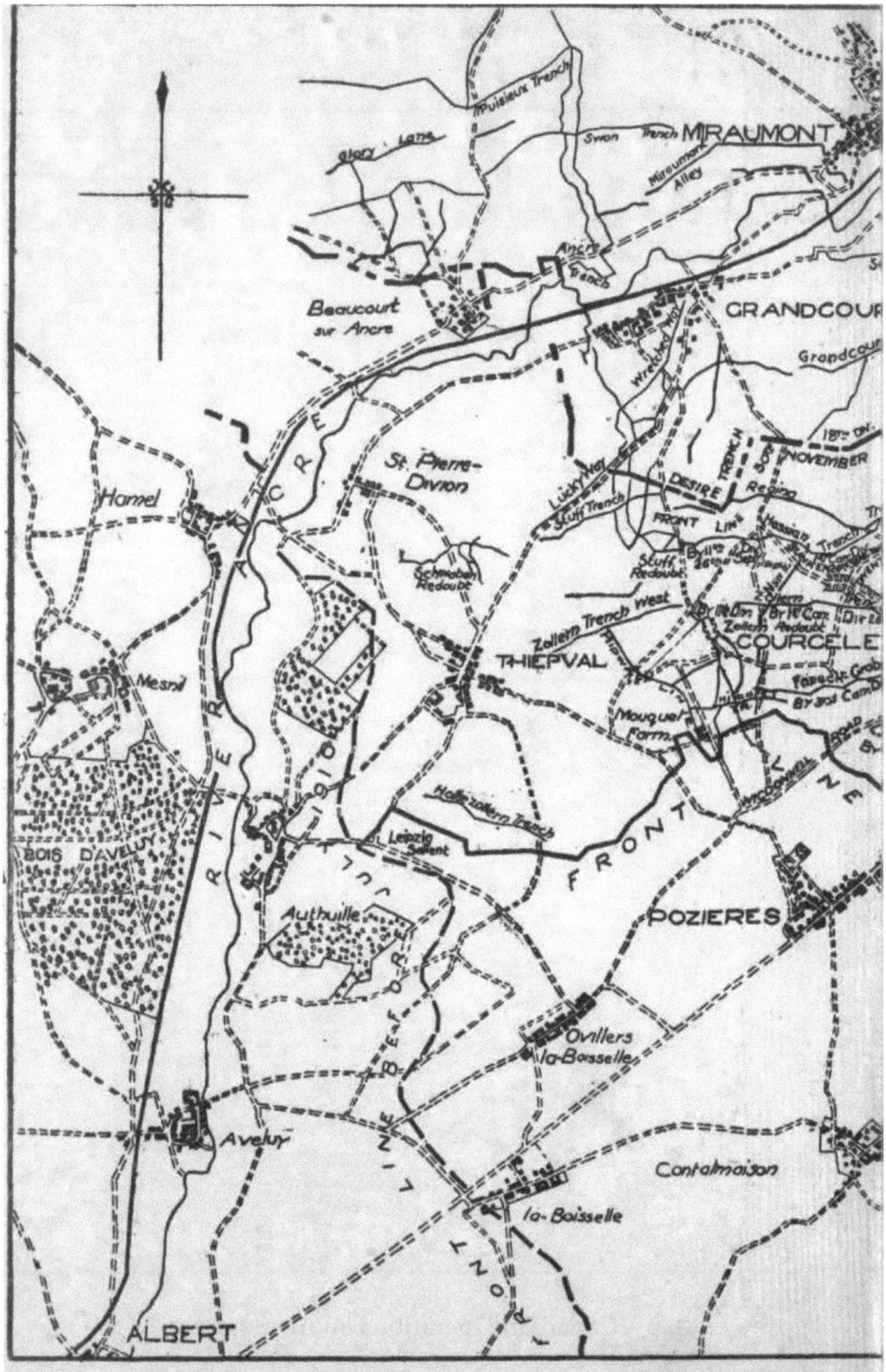

Map—Canadian Operations on the Somme (Enlarged)

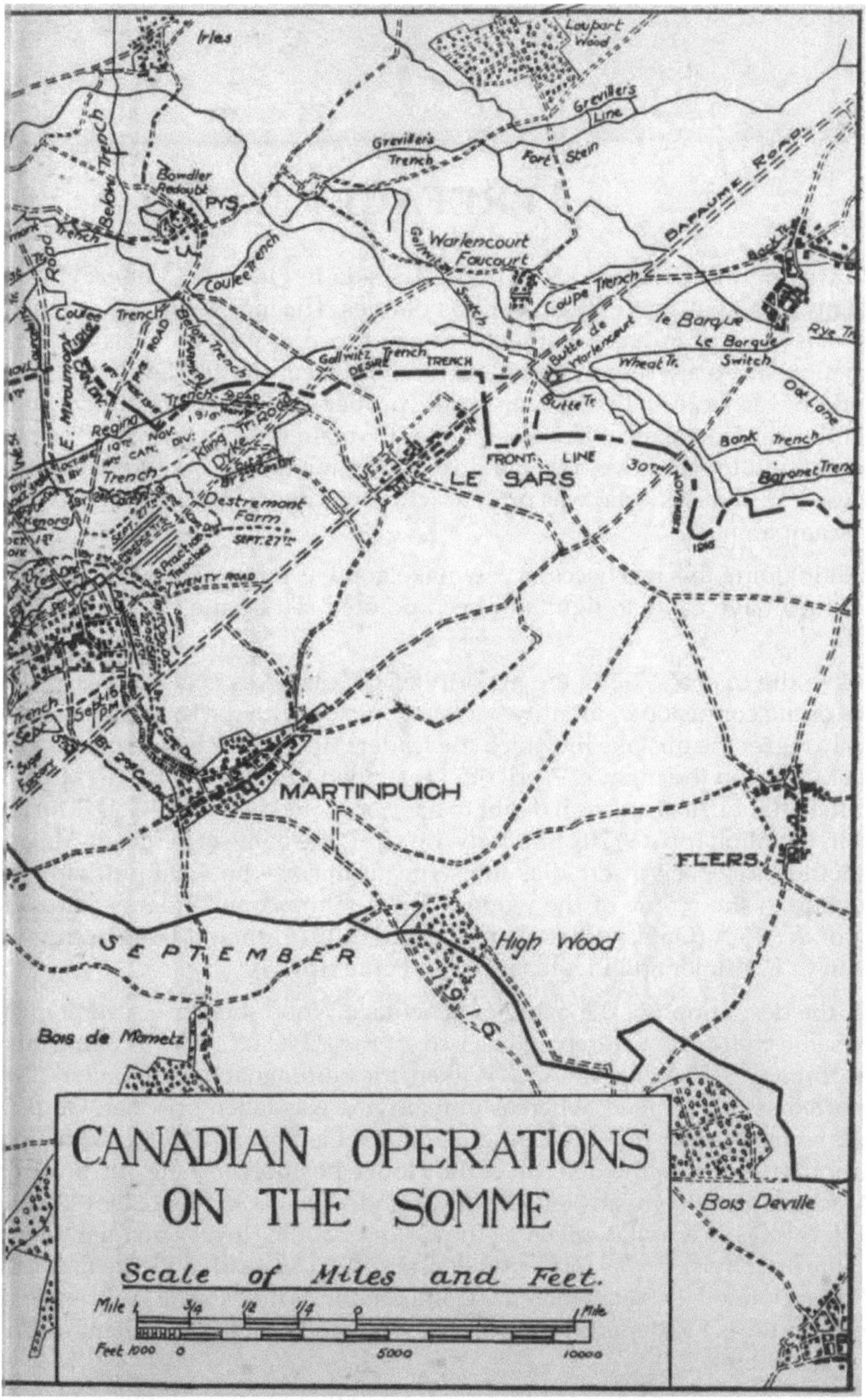

Map—Canadian Operations on the Somme (Enlarged)

PREFACE

In writing this preface to Vol. III of "Canada in Flanders" I am saying good-bye to my task as author of the first two volumes. The increasing pressure of other duties has made it impossible for me to pay those prolonged visits to the Front which alone keep a writer in vivid touch with the constantly developing realities of modern war, or to spare the time for the proper study of the historical material. Under these circumstances it seemed better to retain the Editorship of "Canada in Flanders," but to hand over the story of the Somme to the practised pen of Major Charles G. D. Roberts, who was present with the Canadian Corps during that Autumn Campaign.

But in doing this it is necessary to make good as far as possible the errors and slips which have come to light and been pointed out by the critics in the text of Vol. II.

As in the case of Vol. I., the majority of the mistakes is in the misspelling of names or the confusion of identity between officers with the same surname. I particularly regret the mistake by which the leadership of the advance on the lost craters at St. Eloi on the night of April 6th is ascribed to Lieutenant V. P. Murphy, of the 25th Battalion, instead, as it ought to have been, to Lieutenant G. D. Murphy, of the 28th Battalion (pp. 69, 70). Similarly, on p. 21, the name of Sergeant-Major Benton should have been inserted as the sergeant-major who went out with Private Donoghue to the rescue of the wounded; while the commanders of the raiding party of the 19th (Ontario) Battalion in August, 1916, should have been given as Captain C. E. Kilmer and Lieutenant H. B. Pepler (p. 35).

In the description of the battle of Sanctuary Wood there are several mistakes of the same character. Lieutenant Glassco, of the P.P.C.L.I., has his name misspelt on pp. 97 and 98, and Captain A. G. Wilken, the heroic chaplain of the 1st C.M.R.'s, is reported as being killed, whereas in reality he was taken prisoner. On p. 117 it should be made clear that the Colt guns under Lieutenant Ziegler, which played so important a part in the defence of the Hooge position on June 6th, belonged to the Machine Gun Company of the 7th Brigade. On p. 36 Lieutenant-Colonel C. H. Hill, D.S.O., is wrongly given as the Colonel of the Royal Canadian Regiment when the 3rd Division was formed in January, 1916, instead of Lieutenant-Colonel A. H. MacDonnell, D.S.O.; while the Commander of the 5th C.F.A. Brigade at the same period was Lieutenant-Colonel W. O. H. Dodds, and not Lieutenant-Colonel E. A. Carruthers.

Among more general errors it may be noted that Lieutenant Elliot is described on p. 73 as the "signal" instead of the "signalling" officer, and that the German unit opposed to us at St. Eloi was the 214th Regiment, and not the 214th Battalion—a German regiment consisting of three battalions and approximating more in numbers to our brigade.

On more general questions, such as the position and actions of units, only one controversy has been raised, and that is concerned with the early stages of the Battle of St. Eloi. This difficulty is to some extent inevitable, for with the exception of the Second Battle of Ypres there has been no action in this history of the Corps in which the true facts have been more difficult to obtain than in that confused fighting in the mud on the dreary dawn of April 6th of 1916, which lost us the craters and the advanced line. But all the available evidence has been sifted with the greatest care, and nothing has been brought to my attention which makes me inclined to modify or alter the provisional account given in the second volume. This does not mean in the least that in the future quite fresh material, both from Canadian and German sources, may not become available after the war and throw a totally new light on certain episodes. With this additional evidence before him the future historian may be able to rewrite parts of the story from the standpoint of this fuller knowledge. There is, however, one particular correction which can be made at once. I find that I have done something less than justice to the work of the 2nd Pioneer Battalion during the St. Eloi fighting. Their task here was one of incredible difficulty owing to the conditions of the weather, the state of the ground, to the severe and continuous shelling to which the whole area was subjected, and the uncertainty as to positions which wrapped the whole action in a fog. Yet the Pioneers' work was carried through with great courage and energy. In particular, the reconstruction of the old front British line from Shelley Farm to No. 2 Crater, which is ascribed on p. 77 to the infantry of the 5th Brigade, was in reality done by the Pioneers, who also took a large share in placing No. 2 Crater itself in an adequate state of defence.

There is an inevitable tendency to give to the work of the troops immediately behind the firing-line less attention and credit than they deserve.

The infantry sustain most of the hard knocks when it comes to climbing the parapet, and in return obtain the greater notice from the historian. But behind the thin and scattered lines, which wave after wave fall or go plodding on, the gunners, the sappers, and the pioneers are preparing or consolidating the victory. The battle is no longer between the opposing lines of the infantry, for to win a position you must hold it, and to hold it you must have brought up swiftly and safely from the rear bombs, ammunition, wire rations, and a means of entry for the supporting and relieving troops, the area of the battle is no longer the front line, it is behind this that the enemy barrage descends, and over a wide field of fire the German shells are searching for all those who would bring up succour and relief. It is under these conditions that the pioneers must do their work. In the night, only illumined by the fitful flare of the star-shells shedding a pale and sudden luminance behind the front line and leaving the darkness more intense than ever, the old and battered communication trench of the Germans has to be made good to the front line. The trench from previous occupation is well known to the enemy, and as the pioneers shovel out the mud and the dirt to the left and right a new illumination is provided by the sudden glare and suffocating fumes of the heavies bursting right or left or in the trench itself. But night at least gives the appearance, if not the reality, of safety. As the infantry go forward the work must often be done in the broad daylight, the trench driven through to the new line, or a new resistance built to face the counter-attack. The men of the Pioneers who have to undertake this task must do it in cold blood. They are robbed of that excitement of personal conflict which can carry the fighting man through the most desperate dangers in a frame of mind which hardly remembers the horrors through which he passes, and crowns the story of his achievements with a halo and a fascination not granted to work less interesting but no less vital.

The achievements of the 2nd Pioneer Battalion at the Somme will take rank with any of those of the infantry. At Courcelette their duty was to follow on the heels of the 2nd Division, to drive communication trenches through without delay to the new lines, and to relieve the infantry immediately of the final consolidation of the captured trenches. In the darkness before the assault Lieutenants McGhee and Davis crawled out into No Man's Land and pegged out the line of trenches to be dug next day. The moment the 2nd Division had taken the German front line the Pioneers started out to drive these trenches through in broad daylight and under a sweeping rain of heavies. Lieutenant McGhee exhibited great courage and devotion to duty; he was three times buried by the explosion of heavy shells close to him, and three times dug himself out with his entrenching tool and continued to mark out the line of the advancing trench for his men. What the effect of such shelling may be is illustrated by the extraordinary and gruesome story of the death of Lieutenant Tracy of the same regiment some days before. While prospecting in advance of the line a German shell burst right on him. A rescue party of Pioneers went out immediately to find him on the spot of the shell-burst. Not a sign of the unfortunate officer could be found, and the search was abandoned. On the day of Courcelette his body was found by the advancing infantry fifty yards from where he had been struck down. For the Pioneers this kind of work must be done, day in and day out, or night in and night out, for weeks at a time. When the infantry is too exhausted by its efforts to make good the line, the Pioneers must be called up to supplement their efforts. If a strong point has to be built, it is to the Pioneers that the engineer officer will look to carry out his instructions, and in the achievement of all these tasks the Pioneer Battalions of the Canadians have covered themselves with glory.

It is now my duty to hand over to my successor. Major Charles G. D. Roberts continues in Vol. III. of Canada in France and Flanders, for France has now given us the names of the Somme and of Vimy, the story of the Autumn Campaign of 1916. I retire gladly in favour of one who has a real claim to literary and historical fame. The first and second volumes were the hasty product of one who was an amateur in the art of describing, but who, as an amateur, did his best. Major Roberts is a professional in the sphere of letters and of history, and therefore sets up a new and higher standard for the volumes which are to follow. In the sphere of letters he is well known throughout the Empire for his stories of the life of the men and the denizens of the wild, through which there blows, like the breeze shaking the pine-trees in the snows, both the warm wind of romance and the cold breath of reality. His History of the Dominion is equally familiar to all Canadians who care to consult the past of their country. In his record of the great deeds of the Canadian Corps on the Somme we shall find combined the two qualities which make letters last, the imagination which can convey to the future the agonies and heroisms of the past, and the chiselled style shaping the rough outlines of the records into a clean-cut and enduring narrative.

BEAVERBROOK.

Cherkley, 1918.

CONTENTS

CHAPTER X

CHAPTER I

THE FOURTH DIVISION

In the first and second volumes of this history Lord Beaverbrook has told the war-story of Canada from the mobilisation of the 1st Canadian Division at Valcartier in August, 1914, to the conclusion of our work in the Ypres salient in June, 1916. He has dealt progressively with from one to three divisions, bringing the second and third in turn into his narrative, recording the organisation of each as it came into being, and then co-ordinating its military exploits with the exploits of its sister divisions.

During all that time the 4th Canadian Division was on its way. It was struggling into existence. Its battalions were forming, training, being reduced to skeletons by the necessities of the veteran units in France, and recovering strength by the absorption of raw material. The 44th Battalion was mobilised in the winter of 1915, while the 1st Division was still on Salisbury Plain; yet it was not until the autumn of 1916 that it reached France as a unit of the 4th Canadian Division. Between the date of its mobilisation and that of its first contact with the enemy it supplied many drafts of officers and men to reserve and fighting battalions in England and France, and absorbed drafts of all ranks from junior units. It was so with all the infantry battalions which, in time, went to the composition of the new Division, only to a lesser degree than in the case of the 44th.

Of the infantry brigades of this Division only the 10th is of purely Western origin, its battalions—the 44th, 46th, 47th, and 50th—having been recruited in Winnipeg, Southern Saskatchewan, British Columbia, and Calgary respectively. These battalions had comprised the 14th (Reserve) Canadian Infantry Brigade during their period of training in England previous to the formation of the 4th Division. The brigade sailed for France on August 10th, 1916, and took a place in the front line for the first time twelve days later, when it relieved our 4th Brigade in a section of our tortured defences before Ypres.

During the first five months of its active service the 10th was commanded by Brigadier-General W. St. Pierre Hughes. On January 18th, 1917, it was taken over by Brigadier-General Edward Hilliam, D.S.O., late C.O. of the 25th Battalion. The story of this Brigade's offensive and defensive operations is to be found in subsequent chapters of this history incorporated in the general narrative of Canadian activities.

The 11th Canadian Infantry Brigade, organised in May, 1916, lost two of its original battalions in the following month, owing to the great and immediate need of reinforcements at the front in consequence of the bitter fighting of June in the Ypres salient. These units were replaced by others; and when it commenced its actual war-service it consisted of the 54th from Kootenay, the 75th from Toronto, the 87th of Montreal, and the 102nd of Northern British Columbia. This Brigade was originally commanded by Brigadier-General F. O. W. Loomis, D.S.O., who had previously commanded a battalion of the 1st Canadian Division; but after Major-General Mercer was killed in action in June, the 2nd Brigade contributed its G.O.C., Major-General Lipsett, to the 3rd Division, Loomis was recalled to France to take the 2nd Brigade, and Lieutenant-Colonel V. W. Odlum, D.S.O., of the 7th Battalion, was promoted to the command of the 11th Brigade and the rank of Brigadier-General.

The 12th Canadian Infantry Brigade was organised from the 16th (Reserve) Brigade in May, with Brigadier-General Lord Brooke in command. It originally consisted of the 51st, 72nd, 73rd, and 87th Battalions, but in June twenty-four officers and more than seven hundred other ranks of the 51st were drafted to France, and their place in the Brigade was filled by the 78th. The 87th was transferred to the 11th Brigade. The final composition of the 12th Brigade was as follows:—38th Battalion of Ottawa (its *personnel* representing such well-known Canadian Militia regiments as the Governor-General's Foot Guards, the Duke of Cornwall's Own Rifles, the Brockville Rifles, the Lanark and Renfrew Regiment and the Stormont and Glengarry Highlanders), the 72nd Battalion of Vancouver, the 73rd of Montreal, and the 78th of Winnipeg.

Shortly after its arrival in France the command of the 12th Canadian Infantry Brigade was transferred to Brigadier-General J. H. MacBrien, D.S.O.

From the date of its organisation the 4th Canadian Division has been commanded by Major-General David Watson, C.B.

This Division has been fortunate from the first in the matter of the *personnel* of its higher commands and senior appointments. Major-General Watson commenced his military service in this war in August, 1914, as a Lieutenant-Colonel. He did splendid work with his battalion—the 2nd (Central Ontario)—during the Second Battle of Ypres and until he was promoted to the command of the 5th Brigade in the autumn of 1915.

Brigadier-General Edward Hilliam, who took over the command of the 10th Brigade in January, 1917, has had a career of distinguished activity since the first day of Canada's military participation in the war. As a Captain of the 5th Battalion he was wounded at Gravenstafel Ridge on April 25th, 1915, while engaged on a service of exceptional danger and importance. The story is told in Vol. I. of this history. After months more of hard service with the 5th, and a step in rank, he was promoted Lieutenant-Colonel and transferred to the 25th (Nova Scotia) Battalion. His success continued unfalteringly with his new command, as the splendid work of the Nova Scotians at Courcelette on September 15th, 1916, has proved to the world.

Brigadier-General Loomis, who commanded the 11th Brigade for a time in England, is another survivor of the Second Battle of Ypres. His original battalion was the 13th Royal Highlanders of Canada. From the 11th Brigade he was recalled to France in June, 1916, to command the 2nd Brigade. His Brigade-Major, Captain Gardner, a veteran of the 7th Battalion, returned to France at the same time and took over the 7th from Lieutenant-Colonel Odlum, who was appointed to the command of the 11th Brigade.

Brigadier-General V. W. Odlum, D.S.O., before his promotion to a brigade had commanded the 7th (British Columbia) Battalion at the front since the death of Lieutenant-Colonel Hart-McHarg in April, 1915. To those who know, this statement sufficiently explains Odlum's fitness for any fighting command.

Brigadier-General J. H. MacBrien, commanding the 12th Brigade, was at one time D.A.A. and O.M.G. of the 1st Canadian Division, and in recognition of his services in this capacity he was mentioned in despatches and made a Companion of the Distinguished Service Order. He was afterwards promoted to the General Staff of the Canadian Corps.

Lieutenant-Colonel W. E. Ironsides, D.S.O., Major K. D. B. Murray, D.S.O., and Captain A. A. Aitken, General Staff officers, first, second, and third grade of the Division, all have served actively on one or more of Britain's fighting fronts since the first days of the war. Captain R. M. Redmond was drawn from the Casualty Centre after he had seen service with the 60th Battalion of the 3rd Division. All other officers of the Divisional Staff had seen previous service in France, and a number of them had been decorated for their good work. By hard work or hard fighting Lieutenant-Colonel E. B. Panet, Colonel H. A. Chisholm, and Captain F. R. Burnside had won the D.S.O., and Captain Meurling and Hon. Major the Reverend A. M. Gordon the Military Cross, long before the materialisation of the 4th Canadian Division.

The 3rd Canadian Divisional Artillery, which was organised and trained in England during the spring and summer of 1916, and went to France with the 4th Division, consists of the 8th, 9th, 10th, and 11th Canadian Artillery Brigades and the Divisional Artillery Ammunition Column. The batteries and sections of which this force was formed came originally from almost every corner of Canada, north and south, east and west.

For a time the Brigades were composed as follows:—The 8th, of the 30th, 31st, 40th, and 41st Field Batteries; the 9th, of the 32nd, 33rd, 45th, and 46th Field Batteries; the 10th, of the 37th, 38th, 39th, and 44th Field Batteries; and the 11th (Howitzer) Brigade of the 29th, 35th, 36th, and 43rd Howitzer Batteries. This organisation was not satisfactory. The 29th (Howitzer) Battery was left with the 11th Brigade, and to it were added the 41st, 44th, and 46th Field Batteries. To replace these field batteries in the other Brigades the 35th (Howitzer) Battery went to the 8th, the 36th to the 9th, and the 43rd to the 10th. Thus each Brigade was composed of three field batteries and one howitzer battery.

The 8th Brigade, Canadian Field Artillery, which was brought from Canada to England by Lieutenant-Colonel Gillies, passed into the hands of Lieutenant-Colonel D. T. V. Eaton, of the Royal Canadian Horse Artillery, on March 9th, 1916. Eaton had commanded the R.C.H.A. with our 1st Division in France in 1915. He is a professional as well as a practical artillery officer, with years of theoretical and scientific study behind his experience in the field.

The command of the 9th Brigade, C.F.A., went to Lieutenant-Colonel H. G. Carscallen, who had long ago been mentioned in despatches for his work at the Front with the 11th Battery; that of the 10th to Lieutenant-Colonel G. H. Ralston, who distinguished himself as far back as June, 1915, at the "Duck's Bill," when two guns of his battery were established and fought in our front-line trench, seventy-five yards distant from the German trench, with disastrous results to the enemy's wire, parapets, and machine-gun emplacements (see Vol. I., p. 77). Lieutenant-Colonel A. G. MacNaughton, late of the 2nd Brigade, C.F.A., was appointed to the 11th Brigade.

These four Brigades and their ammunition column went to France under the command of Brigadier-General J. H. Mitchell, late of the 3rd Brigade, C.F.A. This officer had been mentioned in despatches and awarded the Legion of Honour, Croix d'Officier, a year before.

The 4th Canadian Division went to France in August, 1916, the 10th Infantry Brigade arriving on the 11th, the 11th Brigade on the 14th, and the 12th Brigade on the 15th. On the 17th they assembled, and within the week were moved into positions on the war-torn front of the Ypres salient. There they remained until the first week in October, when they joined the Canadian Corps on the Somme. During their occupation of the Ypres salient each of the three Brigades was withdrawn in turn for a course of tactical training.

So it was that the autumn of 1916 saw the Canadian Army in France flooding to and beyond the one hundred thousand mark. Four Divisions, according to the old establishment, which gave twenty-two thousand men of all ranks and arms to a division, would account for eighty-eight thousand Canadians in France at that time, but the development of the machine-gun service and the creation of trench-mortar batteries long ago caused the outgrowth and consequent revision of that establishment. And still, without the addition of a further Division, the Canadian Army Corps continued to grow, waxing greater daily to meet every progressive need and condition of modern warfare. By January, 1917, Canada's man-power in France reached the significant total of one hundred and twelve thousand. This figure takes no account of the wastage of battle. The seriously wounded and work-worn who are returned to England are, like the dead, immediately struck out of the tally. This figure stands for fit Canadians actively employed at the moment in first-hand combat with the enemy.

In the past, great battles have been won and long wars brought to a swift and violent end, tyrants have been broken, races enslaved, and thrones overturned by armies far weaker in numbers and in spirit than these fighting legions of Canada.

To enforce the significance of this Canadian Field Army of 112,000, we may compare the numbers engaged in some of the decisive battles of the past. The army of Napoleon, for instance, numbered but 70,000 men when he broke the power of Austria and Russia at Austerlitz. Wellington won the crushing victory of Vittoria, in the Peninsular War. with a force of 65,000; and at Waterloo he commanded rather less than 68,000. The terrific battle of Gettysburg, in the American Civil War, was fought by 78,000 Federals against the slightly smaller forces of the Southern Confederacy. Even at the great battle of Sedan, which decided the issue of the Franco-Prussian War in 1870, the army of France, on which all her hopes were staked—and lost—numbered but 150,000. From such figures may be estimated the importance of Canada's contribution in the present gigantic struggle for liberty and right.

In the summer of 1914 Canada was a land of peace, of self-interest, of political warfare, and commercial and agricultural prosperity; and now her thousands lie dead on foreign battlefields; thousands of her sons have returned to her, maimed, broken, and blind; her forward army fights on, continually bleeding yet continually growing in strength, reinforced from her trained troops in England; and to her own home camps and garrisons her sons continue to gather from counting-house, school, and farm.

CHAPTER II

HOLDING THE LINE

The Battle of Sanctuary Wood was fought and endured throughout the first two days of June, 1916. Canada's resistance to that terrific and overwhelming onslaught of metal and men will live as long and gloriously as any victory in the great story of our arms. During those two fateful days Canadian trenches were obliterated—blown out of the ground; dug-outs were buried and strong points crushed; woods in our positions were mown and torn to earth; Major-General Mercer was killed and one of our Brigade commanders wounded and taken prisoner. The Canadian front was crushed by that indescribable deluge of exploding metal—but it was not broken.

Between the heroic actions in the Ypres salient in June (1st to 15th) and the commencement of our strenuous thrusts on the Somme front in mid-September, no unit of the Canadian Corps was in any major offensive operation. But the routine work of holding and strengthening our positions continued with the full measure of that activity for which the Canadians have become famous. The vitality of our opposition to the confronting masses of men and machinery did not lessen for an instant. Relieved from the recent terrific efforts of defence and counter-attack, we were stationary yet aggressive. Hostile trenches and strongholds were raided and bombarded, wire was cut by hand and smashed by shell-fire, and mines were sprung. All arms continued to carry on enthusiastically, and the mental peace and physical security of the occupants of opposing positions were shattered constantly by bayonet and grenade, trench-bomb, bullet, and shell. The following instances will serve to illustrate the nature of our activities throughout this period of waiting, of preparation, and of so-called quiet.

Dominion Day (July 1st) was celebrated by the 26th (New Brunswick) Battalion in a manner little appreciated by the grey ranks across the way. Supported by the fire of our artillery and trench-mortars, two officers and twenty-five other ranks operated against a convenient point in the German front-line trench. The assaulting party were observed and subjected to a brisk but inaccurate fire of machine-guns and rifles before they had passed the enemy's inner wire. They pressed forward without a pause and rushed the parapet. The garrison of the trench immediately retired from this threatened point except for three men, who stuck to their loopholes and continued firing. Lieutenant Fleming accounted for one of these by thrusting his revolver into a loophole and returning the fire. The trench was then entered and its remaining defenders disposed of. After our party had investigated about forty yards of the trench they were driven out by a heavy bombardment of rifle-grenades and mortar-bombs. They then returned to our own lines with a few slight casualties, some useful information, and a quantity of German equipment.

An encounter in No Man's Land between a patrol of the 22nd (French Canadian) Battalion and a German patrol on the night of July 4th resulted in the dispersion of the enemy and our capture of two prisoners.

Ten nights later a reconnoitring patrol from the 25th (Nova Scotia) Battalion attacked an enemy listening-post at the moment of its being strongly reinforced. After a brisk exchange of grenades the Germans ran for their trench, leaving the field and one of their wounded to us.

On the night of the 25th a large German mine was blown in our lines on the Bluff. This was not the enemy's first attempt to possess himself of that advantageous position. It will be remembered that he attained his object in January of the same year and was not driven out until a month later, and then only at a heavy cost of killed and wounded. Fortunately the second attempt to secure a foothold on that ground failed utterly, thanks to the alertness and prompt action of our troops immediately concerned. Briefly, the story of the foiled effort is this:—

The 1st Canadian Division, which had taken over the Bluff sector on the 22nd of the month, received warning two days later from Major North, of the 1st Canadian Tunnelling Company, that the enemy might be depended upon to blow a mine very soon somewhere in the vicinity. The localities which were considered with the liveliest suspicion were a point known as the Bean and Trench 33. The Division immediately warned the 2nd Infantry Brigade of the menace; the G.O.C. the Brigade ordered reductions in the garrisons of the threatened positions, the covering of that section of front by machine-guns, and the detailing of parties for counter-attack and of other parties for the vital work of consolidation should a mine be blown.

The early hours of the night of the 25th were unusually quiet about the Bluff. Artillery was silent. Snipers and machine-gunners seemed half-hearted in their activities. The 7th (British Columbia) Battalion was engaged in preparing for a relief which was to be completed by midnight.

At ten o'clock the quiet was shattered by a tremendous convulsion. Earth, fire, rock, and smoke belched to heaven. Trenches vanished, engulfed. Instantly the S.O.S. rocket went up. Our machine-guns responded like crackling echoes of the explosion.

Within thirty seconds of the rocket-signal for help the guns of Dodd's Group commenced a crushing bombardment of the German positions which threatened the new crater. Our counter-attacking parties advanced, armed with rifles, grenades, and machine-guns. They occupied the forward lip of the crater, the flanking shell-holes overlooking its raw depths, certain points commanding the canal, and a ridge running between an historic old crater and the new.

The Germans, reinforced and ready for the dash from cover and the occupation of the Crater swarmed to their parapets, and swayed and seethed there for a little while like a headed wave about to break and flood forward. Then the wave broke and subsided—backward instead of forward.

The great attack was dead, dead in the first half-minute of its furious and painful life, killed by the smashing fire of our artillery and the whipping hail of our machine-guns.

Within one and a half hours of the blowing of the mine the O.C. the 7th Battalion reported to his Brigadier that the menace was past, and that the new crater was being swiftly absorbed by our defensive positions. Our artillery reduced its fire by one-half. Five minutes later the German artillery retaliation ceased, the fire of our machine-guns and artillery dropped to normal, and the relief of our infantry—which had been interrupted and delayed for nearly two hours—was calmly continued.

Owing to the precaution of thinning the garrisons in the threatened locality, our casualties were wonderfully light—less than fifty all told in killed, wounded, and missing. It is safe to say that the enemy casualties, caused by our artillery, machine-guns, Stokes and trench-mortar batteries, were much heavier; and, in addition to their loss of life and limb, the Germans lost their adventure. The months of toil devoted to the laying of the mine and the tons of explosive which comprised it failed to strengthen their position by a tittle or to weaken ours by a jot.

On the night of the 28th a patrol from the Nova Scotian Battalion (25th), consisting of a lieutenant, a sergeant, and four men, carried out a daring raid on a small scale. They bombed the German trench at the point where they intended to enter, and were about to negotiate the parapet when a party of eight enemy bombers attacked them on the flank. In the brief but desperate fight which followed this unexpected distraction three of the Canadians were wounded and the eight Germans were disposed of. Lieutenant Wise, with Sergeant Anderson and Private Johnson, then entered the hostile trench and discovered that their preliminary grenade-fire had killed five of the garrison. They drove the enemy down the trench, until Anderson was wounded. Lieutenant Wise ceased his offensive to help the sergeant over the parapet, and while thus engaged he received three wounds. Johnson continued to drive the enemy until all his grenades were thrown. He then escaped from the trench, returned to our lines, collected a rescue party, and led the way back to the scene of action. All our wounded were found and brought in with the exception of Sergeant Anderson.

At half-past eight on the morning of the 29th the 19th (Ontario) Battalion made a daylight raid into the enemy trenches on the St. Eloi front between Ruined Farm and the Canal. Two officers and the scouts of the Battalion had devoted every day and night of the preceding week to reconnoitring the ground over which the attack was to be made. During the night of the 28th the enemy's wire in front of the point selected for entry was hand-cut by two men of the Battalion. Machine-gun fire on the hostile parapet at the threatened point muffled the sound of the clipping of the wire. The raiding party, consisting of Captain C. L. Kilmer Lieutenant H. B. Pepler, and eighteen N.C.O.'s and men, covered three-quarters of their journey between the lines by way of an old ditch, doubled across the remaining forty-five yards, passed through the gaps in the wire, and went over the parapet before they were discovered by the enemy. They moved to the right and left along the trench, shooting and bombing. Upon the approach of strong German reinforcements along a communication trench, the signal to retire was given and successfully obeyed. During the evacuation of the trench the raiders suffered a few slight casualties from grenade-fire, and the two officers and a sergeant sustained shrapnel wounds. Captain Kilmer was the last to leave the trench. One of his ankles had been broken in the fight. As he was unable to reach our lines unassisted, and unwilling to delay the retirement, he crawled into a shell-hole situated about eight yards in front of the German wire. He was rescued from this insecure retreat by Lieutenant Burnham, Corporal Wilson, and Private Newton, who, covered by an accurate barrage from the guns of Stewart's Group, moved out to the shell-hole and back to our lines under a heavy fire of machine-guns and rifles.

In this, the first of our daylight raids, no prisoners were taken. The action was too swift and the encounters were too violent to permit of the removal of a single living Hun; but the operation was highly successful. The occupants of the trench were identified as the Royal Württembergers; valuable information of a technical nature was obtained; two machine-guns were put out of action and other machine-gun and trench-mortar emplacements located; many of the garrison of the trench were shot, and four large dug-outs, crowded with men, were effectively bombed; and it is reasonable to suppose that the casualties inflicted by our artillery were severe. Lieutenant H. R. Dillon, Canadian Field Artillery, who acted as Forward Observation Officer throughout the operation, did splendid service, especially during the rescue of Captain Kilmer, when he stood fully exposed in No Man's Land at a point within forty yards of the German trench, and from there directed the fire of his battery. Lieutenant Hooper, of the 19th Battalion, whose active command during the raid included a Lewis gun, snipers, and a telephonist, also did fine work.

On the night of August 5th-6th the 27th (City of Winnipeg) Battalion sent a raiding party into the enemy trenches opposite their front, with the usual objects of obtaining prisoners and information and inflicting casualties. This raid was daringly executed; but the fighting in the trench was so severe that no prisoners were taken. Lieutenant Harris was wounded while carrying a wounded German toward the point of entry. Two unwounded Germans were caught, but owing to their struggles and the depth of the trench the efforts of their captors to expel them over the parapet were ineffectual.

Eight nights later Lieutenant Clarkson of this same Battalion led another party into the enemy's lines and succeeded in bringing out a prisoner. The garrison of the invaded trench suffered heavily. Of Clarkson's party only one man was wounded.

A party from the 28th (North-West) Battalion, supported by the artillery of Stuart's Group, our trench-mortars, and Stokes guns, entered the enemy's trenches in the neighbourhood of Ruined Farm on the night of August 10th-11th. Lieutenant T. L. O. Williams, who commanded the raiders, was wounded. The enemy and his trenches were severely knocked about and a prisoner was brought back.

A dummy raid on the hostile positions at the Hollandscheschuur Farm and Quarante Wood salients was successfully practised by Dodd's Group, C.F.A., and the 10th (Ontario) Battalion in the early hours of August 15th. The object of this long-headed enterprise was to draw the Germans in force into their front-line trenches and there drub them thoroughly with the combined fire of our field batteries, Stokes guns, and machine-guns.

At 3.45 a.m. three white flares were sent up from our lines, and at the same time the enemy's entanglements were violently shaken by means of strong wires which connected them with our forward positions. The Germans immediately took alarm and subjected their own entanglements to a heavy grenade bombardment along the whole front from the Quarante Wood to the Chemin de Poperinghe. Our artillery and Stokes guns then opened heavily and accurately on selected targets on the enemy front and support trenches. The Germans promptly attempted a retaliation with the fire of a five-point-nine battery; but as their first two shells fell in their own lines at the Farm, the third in No Man's Land, and the next thirty-seven on various points behind and in their own defences, they soon became discouraged.

In addition to the casualties and material damage inflicted by our fire, the enemy must have suffered heavily from the erratic performance of his own five-point nines.

On the 17th a new strong point in the system of enemy trenches known as "the Loop," in Sanctuary Wood, about two thousand yards east of Zillebeke, was subjected to a concentrated bombardment by our 6-inch howitzers and partially destroyed. To complete its destruction the bombardment was resumed during the night of the 17th and 18th, and under cover of this bombardment a raid was undertaken by a party from the Royal Canadian Regiment against an advanced trench sector and bombing post in the immediate neighbourhood of "the Loop." The idea was to take the enemy by surprise while their attention was occupied by the bombardment, and to capture prisoners. In both these respects, however, the operation was a failure, as the Germans were found fully prepared and "standing to," with the post heavily manned, and not only were no prisoners taken, but not one of our men succeeded in getting into the trench. The affair was memorable, however, for the amazing courage and audacity with which it was pushed, in the teeth of overwhelming and ready numbers, and for the resourcefulness and heroic devotion with which the three officers—Lieutenant Bole, leader of the raiding party, and Lieutenants Churchill and Munn, who had come to his assistance—succeeded in bringing all the wounded back to our lines. It was remarkable, too, for the slaughter inflicted in the crowded trench by this greatly daring handful of raiders. The raiding party consisted of sixteen N.C.O.'s and men under Lieutenant Bole. A gap was blown in the enemy wire by the explosion of an ammonal tube. Immediately Lieutenant Bole, who had gathered his men at the head of the sap running outward from our front line, led the way through the broken wire in the hope of gaining the position in one rush. They were met, however, by a storm of bombs and machine-gun fire, and fell rapidly. But even the wounded, if not utterly disabled, kept on hurling their bombs. Lance-Corporal Reynolds, though already hit, succeeded in reaching the enemy's parapet and delivering all his bombs with deadly effect among the packed ranks. Then, finding himself alone, he withdrew, and dropped, with two more wounds, a few yards back from the parapet. By this time every member of the party was down except Lieutenant Bole, who occupied himself calmly with the task of rescuing his wounded. Lieutenant Churchill came to his aid in this, while Lieutenant Munn, taking his Lewis gun out into No Man's Land, played it along the enemy's parapet to keep down their fire. Under cover of this gun, and of a trench-mortar barrage which was presently dropped along the trench, Lieutenant Bole got all his wounded, one by one, back through the sap and into our lines. And so the affair ended—not, indeed, with success, but with great distinction for all concerned, and with the consolation of having exacted a heavy toll in German lives.

It may be in place here to give an interesting instance of the work that was being done by our Tunnelling Companies—work calling for not only great courage and devotion, but also the highest technical skill and resource. The work of a tunnelling company at the Front is like a duel with knives in a dark room, where one may feel at any moment the stealthy adversary's knife in one's back. The tunnellers' ears, nerves, and intuition are ceaselessly on the strain. And just when he has successfully mined his opponents and is about to blow them up, he may be counter-mined himself and hurled into eternity. At the position known as "The Bluff," overlooking the Canal, a mine had been blown by the enemy on July 25th, forming a new crater of which we had at once taken possession. By the explosion a lip was formed on the east side of the crater, which was capable of being transformed into an extremely strong position. But it was impossible to work on this position with any degree of safety, as it was certain that the enemy's gallery, from which he had laid the mine, ran somewhere beneath the lip, and was occupied. Any work we should attempt on the position would inevitably be heard in the gallery and could be frustrated, disastrously for us, by the explosion of another mine. It was decided to try to tunnel into the gallery from another direction. Bore-holes, therefore, were driven in the supposed direction of the gallery, in the hope of being able to locate it exactly by listening. In this the borers were so successful that they came upon the gallery before they expected to. The enemy made them aware of their success by exploding a charge beneath the bore-holes, killing three of our men and injuring others. From this, however, it was obvious that the main charge was not yet laid in the gallery. Plans were therefore made at once for endeavouring to sap into the gallery from No Man's Land and blow it in, so as to cut it off at some distance from the crater, and thus, if possible, gain the crater end of it for our own use. In order to begin the work far out in No Man's Land it was absolutely necessary to obtain some cover there, and cover of such a nature that the enemy should not recognise its purpose. The problem might well have seemed an insurmountable one; but Major North, O.C. 1st Tunnelling Company, Canadian Engineers, solved it successfully, outwitting the Germans by an ingenious ruse. In the words of the Official Report:—"One hundred pounds of ammonal were taken over the parapet, and, after a rather difficult reconnaissance, were placed about fifty feet in front of the new crater.... This charge was wired back to *Thames Street*. In co-operation with the 5th Battalion, two 60-pound trench-mortars were fired at the German line in front at a prearranged time, and at one minute interval. A minute later our charge was exploded, and after another minute another trench-mortar was fired, the object being to make the enemy believe that our charge was a trench-mortar fallen short. This charge made a crater about 4 ft. deep and about 8 ft. in diameter, breaking the tough surface layer of roots and gravel. We entered the crater immediately after it was blown, placed another charge of 200 pounds of ammonal, and blew it. The next night we entered the crater, finding it about 8 ft. deep and about 25 ft. in diameter." From this effective cover our boring went on unsuspected, and a number of charges were laid in different bore-holes close to where the gallery was judged to run. When these were simultaneously exploded our calculations were proved correct. A sector of the gallery was found completely wrecked, effectually cutting the communications, and we entered into possession of the undamaged portion, about 112 ft. in length, extending up into the new crater. We thus secured a valuable post of vantage from which to conduct other mining operations, and the crater was consolidated into a strong point of considerable importance to our line.

By these and many similar small operations the enemy were kept at a tension and subjected to continual harassing annoyance; and our own men were encouraged and stimulated while perfecting themselves in the art of modern war.

CHAPTER III

ON THE SOMME

It is around the part played by the Canadian Forces in the gigantic and long-drawn-out struggle known as "the Battle of the Somme" that the interest of this third volume of our records must centre. The operations which began, on July 1st, 1916, with the ponderous thrusts of the British and French Armies from before Albert and Bray, and ended with the capture of Bapaume and Peronne on March 17th and 18th, 1917, constituted, according to the nomenclature of war before these days of Armageddon, not one battle, indeed, but a campaign of many great battles. In this war, however, all is on a scale so colossal that standards and terms of comparison have to be enlarged in due proportion. All that unparalleled outpouring of agony and splendour, of sacrifice and endurance, of heroism and destruction, which the Germans have so poignantly—and significantly—designated as "the blood-baths of the Somme," may be taken as one battle, a battle in whose vast rhythm the old values of hours and days are supplanted by weeks and months. Yet never before in the world's history was there a battle in which minutes have been held so priceless, the seconds themselves so reckoned upon with meticulous precision. To present an adequate picture of the battle as a whole, or even of the specific part played in it by this or that particular corps, is a task that will tax the powers of the inspired historian, viewing the great subject at such a distance that he can see it as a whole and in its true perspective. He will need to be a new Thucydides, equipped, not only with grasp and vision, but also with mastery of the magic of words. And even so, the story will never be half told. Men will continue digging into the records and unofficial accounts as an inexhaustible mine, forever discovering new jewels of wonder and terror and pity. The utmost that can be attempted in this unpretending narrative is to set down the salient facts as to the achievements of our own Divisions, with such detail as can be sifted out, more or less at hazard, while the dust of the stupendous conflict is still in the air.

On September 1st the Canadians began to move from their sector of comparative calm toward the vortex of the gigantic struggle, which was at this period raging with special fury around Mouquet Farm and over the blood-soaked undulations between Pozières, Courcelette, and Martinpuich. The quality of our troops, and the estimation in which they were held by the Higher Command, may be judged by the fact of their being allotted to this vital area, which included the key positions on the direct road to Bapaume. How they justified this confidence, and at what a cost, the sequel will show.

The 1st Canadian Division, General Currie's veterans of Ypres, was the first to move south, and its headquarters were shifted to Rubempré, a few kilometres due west from shell-torn Albert. On the 3rd we find certain battalions supporting the Australians at Tom's Cut; and by the 4th the whole division had moved up through Albert and out along the Bapaume road into the stress of the conflict, taking over from the 4th Australian Division under heavy shell-fire, a hotly-contested line of trenches running from a little behind Mouquet Farm to the junction of Munster Alley with Cameron and Highland trenches, about a mile to the south of Courcelette. On the following day the headquarters of the Division were transferred from Rubempré to the precarious shelters and dug-outs of Tara Mill, on the Bapaume Road, near the grim collections of calcined rubble which had been La Boiselle and Ovillers. On the 6th the 1st Canadian Divisional Artillery arrived, and took over from the 2nd Australian Divisional Artillery in support of General Currie's line. All the time, from the moment of their arrival, our troops were kept under a very destructive bombardment from 5.9, 8-inch, and 11-inch guns, the enemy hoping thus to shake their morale before they could get settled into their new positions; and the communication trenches were so effectively blotted out that the front line could only be reached by going overland. The relief was no more than satisfactorily completed when the war-worn old Division was given a chance to show that its mettle had not deteriorated in the transfer from "the Salient" to the Somme.

In the early morning of the 8th an exposed section of our front trench, about seventy-five yards in extent, held by Lieutenant G. B. Murray, of the 14th Battalion, with Lieutenant B. L. Cook and twenty-four other ranks under his command, was attacked with the bayonet by some two hundred of the enemy, who succeeded at the first rush in forcing their way into the position. The little party of defenders, however, held their ground with bomb, rifle, and cold steel till reinforcements came up, whereupon the assailants were expelled with heavy loss. On the following day came the opportunity which the tried and seasoned Division was waiting for. But it came to one Battalion only—the "Fighting Second" from Eastern Ontario, commanded by Lieutenant-Colonel A. E. Swift, D.S.O.

At exactly twenty-five minutes past one in the afternoon of September 9th, the 2nd Battalion relieved the 4th along the sector of trench, on the right of the Canadian position, from which the attack was to be made. Some 250 yards to the front, south-east of the Windmill on Bapaume Road and near the northern extension of the trench called Walker Avenue, was a blunt salient of German trench, 550 yards or so of it, which was strongly held and proving a thorn in our side. It hung doggedly and defiantly athwart our plans for the advance on Courcelette, a mile away to the north. It was this blunt salient that the "Fighting Second" had been appointed to bite off in order to clear the way for greater enterprises. At a quarter to five precisely the first wave of our attack went over the parapet behind an intense barrage from all our guns. The first three companies of the Battalion only were engaged in the attack, No. 4 Company being held in reserve close by, in Luxton Trench and Walker Avenue. In spite of the punishment which the Germans had been receiving from our barrage, the assaulting wave encountered a sturdy resistance when it reached its objective, and for a few minutes the enemy trench was a pandemonium of savage hand-to-hand struggles with bomb and bayonet. It was a reversion to the ancient form of individual fighting, when great issues so often hung upon the personal prowess of this or that one hero. In this mad encounter individual heroism was too universal to admit of particularisation, but the exploit of Corporal Clarke lifts itself into prominence even in that splendid company. Attacking with a squad of bombers on the extreme left of the wave, he jumped into the trench and found himself alone among a swarm of extremely lively and unsubdued Germans. With the remainder of his bombs he cleared a way for himself. Then with his revolver he accounted for eighteen opponents, two of them being officers, and found himself undisputed master of two bays of the trench. Even more splendid, perhaps, by reason of its self-sacrificing devotion, was the action of Lieutenant Pringle. Leading his platoon against the centre of the enemy's line, he caught sight of a machine-gun hurriedly being mounted on the parapet in such a position that it would be able to wipe out his platoon. Pushing forward at top speed through the storm of shell and bullets, he threw himself single-handed upon the gun-crew before they could get their deadly weapon into action. It never came into action. His men, following close behind, found his body sprawled across the muzzle of the gun, with the crew lying dead around him. Along the rest of the sector the fighting fervour of our men was not to be denied, and the survivors of the enemy presently flung up their hands. In just twenty-two minutes from the beginning of the assault the whole objective was in our hands, 138 prisoners had been gathered in, and the second, or consolidating, wave of the attack was settling itself to the task of making secure the captured position, reversing parapets and firing-step, and commencing new communication trenches back to the old line under the continuing shelter of our barrage. In the meantime, the assaulting wave, taking their Lewis guns with them, moved on and occupied a strong line of shell-holes in front of the trench, while the bombing parties, in the face of desperate opposition, fought their way along the trench and established their blocks some sixty yards to either flank. The price of this victory was two officers killed—Lieutenant Pringle and Lieutenant Stuart—and nine wounded, the wounds of three—Major Williams, Major A. E. McLaughlin, and Lieutenant Bishop—later proving fatal; and of other ranks 69 killed and 190 wounded.

In view of the narrow frontage involved in the attack and the small number of troops engaged, this operation must, of course, be classed as a minor one. But by reason of its soundness of conception, the precision and completeness of its execution, and the importance of its bearing upon our enterprise against Courcelette a few days later, it takes rank with affairs of much greater magnitude and renown. It reflects unbounded credit upon the commanding officer Colonel Swift, whose operation orders were remarkable for their clarity, foresight, and exactness of detail, and upon his second-in-command, Major Vanderwater, who led the attack and carried out those orders with such accuracy. The Battalion was congratulated by General Plunier, the Army Commander, on the following day in terms of unusual commendation.

In the meantime, the 2nd and 3rd Canadian Divisions, following hard upon the heels of the 1st, had moved down from the north to Rubempré and La Plouy, close behind the battle area. On the 11th Major-General Turner, V.C., C.B., D.S.O., commanding the 2nd Division, transferred his headquarters to Tara Hill, and assumed command of the sector which had been so ably controlled by General Currie since the 4th. Throughout the nights of the 10th and 11th the 2nd Division was occupied in relieving the 1st Division, the relief being carried out under extremely trying conditions and at the cost of a good many casualties; for not only the line to be relieved, but all the stripped and tortured waste behind it, was swept by an unceasing storm from the German gun positions across the Ancre and around Pys and Warlencourt. Our communication trenches in many places had been pounded out of existence and landmarks obliterated, with the consequence that some platoons went astray in the darkness and the bewildering uproar, and were hours late in reaching their allotted sectors of trench. Moreover, along with their shrapnel and high explosive, the enemy were sending over many gas and tear shells, which added greatly to the strain of the situation. But the nerve of our Battalions refused to be shaken by this stern ordeal. There was no going back, no wavering. By the morning of the 12th the relief had been completed, and our lines were held by fresh units keen for the test which was already being prepared for them.

On this day the 1st Division went into rest camp at Rubempré, and the 3rd Division, under Major-General L. G. Lipsett, C.M.G., moved up to Usna Hill, their arrival being greeted that same night by a furious attack from the Germans at Mouquet Farm. The brunt of this attack was borne by the 2nd Battalion of the Canadian Mounted Rifles. The assaulting waves were hurled back upon their entrenchments after heavy punishment by our machine-guns and Stokes trench-mortars.

And now we come to COURCELETTE—and write the name in capital letters, as it is one of the shining names in the story of Canadian valour. The storming of that heap of ruins which had once been a sunny Picardian village nestling amid its orchards was an achievement which must make its day—September 15th, 1916—for ever memorable in Canadian history. Of course, as the men who fought and won at Courcelette would be the first to protest, the action, splendid as it was, does not stand in the same category with the Second Battle of Ypres. It is necessary, in writing of it, not to let one's sense of proportion be obscured by its brilliancy and completeness. In the final analysis it will show as a great operation perfectly planned, and executed with a courage, swiftness, and thoroughness calling for the highest praise. Even so, it constitutes but a single stride in the great advance known as the Battle of the Somme. Had it failed, the result would not have been disaster to the Somme operations as a whole, but merely a costly, and perhaps depressing, postponement. The Second Battle of Ypres, on the other hand, belongs not to Canada and the Empire alone, but to the world. It must rank among those few outstanding achievements of uncalculated and self-sacrificing heroism which serve as an incentive to noble spirits for all time. There was that of the miraculous about it which startles and grips the imagination. There was that mingling of high tragedy and terror and devotion which purges national pride to the purest patriotism. It tore victory—men hardly know how to this day—from the jaws of overwhelming and seemingly inevitable defeat; and had it failed, who can set a limit to the catastrophe that might well have followed? Finally, at the Second Battle of

Ypres a young nation came suddenly to full manhood through a well-nigh unparalleled initiation of blood and splendour and tears. It is right that the name of YPRES should stand apart, and its imperishable glory not be infringed upon when allotting their meed of praise to other notable operations of the Canadian Forces.

The capture of Courcelette was the pre-eminent achievement of the Canadians during the year 1916. The glory of it belongs to the 2nd Canadian Division, which, under happy augury, fought the battle on the anniversary of its arrival in France. The Division was highly trained and well seasoned to war by a year of strenuous duty in the tormented area of "the Salient." It had learned all the lessons of endurance and defence in the engulfing mud of Flanders, in the holding of shattered trenches against unrelenting shell-fire and obstinate assault. It had played its part with distinction in the grim struggles around St. Eloi and Hooge. When, therefore, it was selected by Sir Julian Byng the G.O.C. the Canadian Corps, for the great thrust against Courcelette, the General felt that he was employing a weapon of tried keenness and temper which could be depended upon neither to turn nor to break in his hand. The result, as will be seen, more than amply justified his confidence.

The capture of Courcelette, it must be borne in mind, was not an isolated operation. It was an enterprise carried out by the Canadian Corps in conjunction with an attack by our Fourth Army, and by the French Army operating on our right, south of the Somme. The battle was fought in two distinct actions, one in the early morning by the 4th and 6th Brigades, the other in the late afternoon and evening by the 5th Brigade. The first, properly speaking, was the action planned for the day, its objective being the capture of the formidable defences known as Sugar Trench and the Sugar Factory, which barred the way to Courcelette itself. It was, indeed, an ample undertaking for one day; but the success of the attack was so swift and overwhelming, and our troops so straining on the leash, that it was decided to thrust on again at once for the greater prize without giving the dishevelled adversary time to recover. The second, and major, portion of the operation, therefore, may be regarded as an improvisation on the battlefield. At 3.30 in the afternoon the order came for the 5th Brigade, which had been held in reserve during the morning advance, to take Courcelette that same day. Brief as was the notice, within two hours the new operation orders had been issued, and officers and N.C.O.'s fully instructed as to their individual duties. At 6.15 a.m. the barrage lifted and the attacking battalions "went over." Before 7.30 p.m. the whole of Courcelette, with some 1,300 prisoners and much booty, was in our hands, and the position was being consolidated. The second phase of the operation, though planned out with such haste, had worked no less smoothly and according to schedule than the first, and had resulted in a success no less decisive. All through the night, and for several days thereafter, the Germans strove, by furious shelling and desperate counter-attacks, to regain the stronghold from which they had been so precipitately expelled. But our troops proved no less dogged in holding on than they had been dashing in attack, and all the enemy's efforts to retrieve his loss resulted only in further loss of ground and further punishment.

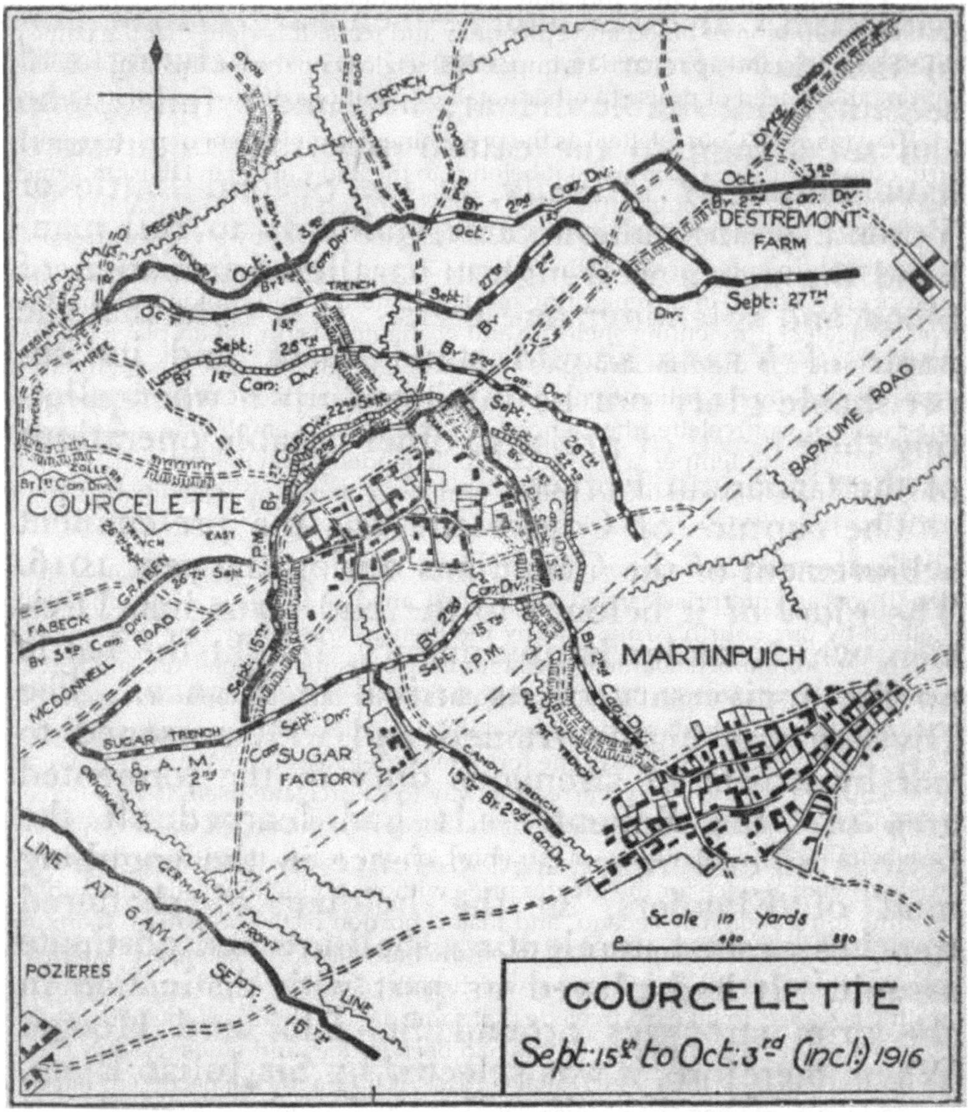

Map—Courcelette Sept. 15th to Oct. 3rd (incl.) 1916

An added interest attaches to the action against Courcelette from the fact that in this engagement appeared for the first time those amazing engines of war known as the "Tanks." The cold official designation of these monsters is simply "Heavy Machine-Gun Battery." But Tommy Atkins, with his fine sense of the fitness of things and his gift for apt nomenclature, could not possibly leave this most daringly original offspring of our military inventiveness to labour under so commonplace a designation. He took this uncouth but invincible ally to his heart at once, and in humorous appreciation christened it a "Tank." And a Tank the amazing creation will remain, except for the purpose of some formal official documents. How effectively the Tanks played their novel *rôle* in the fight for Courcelette will appear in succeeding chapters in course of the detailed account of the individual units involved. Suffice it to say here that the high opinion formed on this, their first appearance, as to the fighting value of this new engine of attack has been more than justified by its later performances, which have confounded the jeers of the pessimist and the sceptic.

CHAPTER IV

THE SUGAR FACTORY AND COURCELETTE

When the Canadians came up to join the struggle on the Somme, they arrived under happy auspices. There was a sense of victory in the air. This is not less true literally than as a figure of speech; for on every hand the clear sky of early autumn in Picardy was dotted by our stationary observation balloons, and threaded by our darting 'planes, which scouted confidently far over the enemy lines or methodically registered for the massed ranks of our guns. Just at this period the supremacy of our Air Service was hardly ever disputed. The German 'planes rarely explored beyond our lines, and the German "sausages" seldom ventured aloft, having learned that such a venture was equivalent to speedy suicide. Moreover, here on the Somme Front our Battalions realised at once that, upon whatsoever hard undertaking they might be launched, they would have the support of an overmastering weight of artillery. Shell-fire, however murderous, loses half its effect upon the men's spirit when they feel that what they are enduring is mild compared to the avalanche of destruction which their own batteries, close behind them, are at the same moment letting loose upon the enemy. Altogether it was a tonic change for our Battalions, after their long gruelling in "the Salient," where at times they had felt themselves in much the position of the toad under the harrow, ground down into the Flanders mire by bombardments from three sides at once, and ceaselessly overlooked by an adversary holding superior positions. Here at last they marched up into the fight over ground wrenched from the enemy in spite of his most deliberate and desperate efforts to hold on to it. Here they felt that they would have a chance to "get a bit of their own back"—and, as the event will show, they got it, full measure and running over.

The terrain over which the attack was to be made is a gently undulating expanse of farm lands stripped naked by the incessant storm of shell-fire and closely pitted with shell-holes and craters. Of grass or herbage not a blade remained, of trees but here and there a bald and riven stump. Dividing this unspeakable waste runs the straight highway from Albert to Bapaume, thick strung with ruined, or rather obliterated, villages. Of these the most advanced in our possession was Pozières, with the great road running directly through it. A mile and a half further on the road runs midway between the twin villages of Courcelette (on the left) and Martinpuich (on the right), which lie about three-quarters of a mile apart. A little nearer our line, and flush with the left of the road—just about a mile from the eastern limit of Pozières—stood a mass of partly demolished brick buildings which had been a great sugar factory, and now, heavily entrenched and fortified by all the arts of the German engineers, constituted the most formidable outpost of Courcelette as well as an important flank defence to the position of Martinpuich. From the western extremity of Martinpuich a strong trench known as Candy Trench ran north-west to the Bapaume Road, skirted the west side of the Sugar Factory, continued in the same direction for a couple of hundred yards past that stronghold, and joined, at right angles, another deeply entrenched and strongly held line called Sugar Trench, which ran south-west for a distance of about twelve hundred yards and ended at McDonnell Road, a second-class thoroughfare almost parallel to the Bapaume highway. It was these two great trenches, each nearly three-quarters of a mile in length, forming two sides of a triangle with the Sugar Factory Fort in the apex, which constituted the grand obstacle to any advance on Courcelette itself. It was an obstacle of the first order, lavishly supported by bombing and machine-gun posts, its flanks fully guarded by trench-works outside of Martinpuich and along McDonnell Road. Such and so formidable was the objective which the 2nd Division set itself out to gain on that memorable morning of the 15th.

The troops detailed for the attack were the 4th and 6th Brigades, the 5th being held in reserve. The position from which the attack was ordered to start was a line of trench covering the front of Pozières, and something under half a mile in advance of the edge of the village. This line, roughly speaking about a mile in extent, ran south-west and north-west across the Bapaume Road, which divided it at right angles into two almost equal sectors, the major sector being that to the north or left of the road. The extreme left of the line rested on McDonnell Road, and joined up at that point with the 3rd Canadian Division. The right connected with the 15th British Division, which lay facing Martinpuich and kept the enemy force there fully occupied. The sector to the right of the Bapaume Road was in the hands of the 4th Brigade, under Brigadier-General R. Rennie, M.V.O., D.S.O., while the left sector was allotted to the 6th, under Brigadier-General H. D. B. Ketchen, C.M.G. The attacking line of the 4th Brigade was made up as follows:—On the right the 18th Battalion (Western Ontario), commanded by Lieutenant-Colonel Milligan; centre, the 20th Battalion (Northern and Central Ontario), commanded by Lieutenant-Colonel C. H. Rogers; and on the left the 21st Battalion (Eastern Ontario), under Lieutenant-Colonel Elmer Jones. In Brigade Reserve was the 24th Battalion (Victoria Rifles of Canada), under Lieutenant-Colonel J. H. Gunn. The attacking line of the 6th Brigade consisted of the 27th Battalion (City of Winnipeg), commanded by Lieutenant-Colonel P. J. Daly, D.S.O.; the 28th (North-West), commanded by Lieutenant-Colonel J. F. Embury, C.M.G.; and the 31st (Alberta), under Lieutenant-Colonel A. H. Bell, with the 29th (Vancouver), familiarly known as Tobin's Tigers, under Lieutenant-Colonel J. S. Tait, in Brigade Reserve. The field guns covering the attack consisted of the 1st Brigade of the 1st Canadian Divisional Artillery and four Brigades of the 18th Divisional Artillery, under Brigadier-General Metcalfe, D.S.O., on the right, and on the left three Brigades of the 1st Canadian Divisional Artillery and one Brigade of the Lahore Artillery, under the command of Brigadier-General Thacker. The barrage work of both these groups throughout the attack was of a closeness and accuracy which left nothing to be desired. It covered both the advance and the consolidation so effectually that our casualty list, though serious, was much smaller than the difficulties of the operation and the strength of the forces opposed to us had permitted us to hope.

The artillery preparation for the attack was begun, by the heavy guns and howitzers, at 1 o'clock in the afternoon of September 14th. From that hour until 3 o'clock in the morning of the 15th the enemy's position was subjected to a deluge of high explosive. At 3 o'clock this fire diminished in intensity. At 4 o'clock it ceased abruptly. A sudden calm fell upon the opposing lines—a calm as full of menace in its sinister suggestiveness, like the core of silence at the heart of the cyclone, as the devouring roar of the bombardment. At the highest pitch of expectation our Battalions waited for the fateful hour of "zero time" creeping up with the dawn.

During this slow hour of waiting, always so stern a test to the nerve of the most seasoned troops, "occurred an incident which"—to quote from Major F. Davy's spirited and picturesque account of the battle—"had it not been promptly met by the vigour and resolution of the Canadians, might have marred, perhaps prevented, the whole attack. A determined attack by a strong enemy bombing party was made upon the right sector of the 4th Brigade front. A portion of the attacking party had actually reached our trenches at the time the attack started. It was overcome by vigorous bombing and rifle fire. A bombing officer in the disputed section, Lieutenant Hugh H. Sykes, 18th Battalion, promptly organised his defence and effectually maintained his position. Lieutenant Gidley, of the 19th Battalion, and parties of bombers from that unit and the 20th Battalion also took part, and frustrated what might have developed into a formidable attack had the initial attempt been successful. The enemy's preparations for this attack eventually told against him, for the strong force he placed in his front trenches to exploit any initial success suffered heavily as our barrage came down upon it."

At dawn of the 15th the air was dry, crisp, and clear—the bite of autumn in it. Patches of pale sky glimmered abundantly between driven fleeces of cloud with promise of fine fighting weather—high visibility, and no baffling obstruction to the work of our airmen. The ground, tossed and furrowed though it was in every direction by the demoniacal ploughshares of the high explosive, gave firm footing—for the curse of the Somme mud had not yet fallen upon our operations. It was such an autumn morning indeed, as to turn men's hearts, with a homesick pang, to the remembrance that this was the date when the hunting season would open in far Canadian woods and swales and coverts. But it was other hunting that opened this day for Canadians on the Bapaume Road—the hunting of the dragon-spawn of treachery and rape.

"Zero hour" had been set for 6.20. At last it came. On the minute—nay, on the second, so exact is now the synchronising of all watches for this work—with a wide-flung, sky-splitting roar our barrage-fire opened. At the same instant all along our front appeared the round, basin-like helmets of the men of our first wave as they climbed over the parapets of the "jumping-off" trenches. Their appearance in itself marked an appreciable gain of ground already secured, for these jumping-off trenches had been dug, with infinite toil and secrecy and at heavy risk, at a distance of 100 to 150 yards in advance of our established front-line trench, by so much shortening the perilous path across the open to our objectives. This arduous and valuable work had been carried out by the 19th Battalion (Toronto and Hamilton) on the right, and by the 29th (Vancouver) on the left.

At four minutes past zero time the barrage lifted to a line about 100 yards farther on, and in another minute our first waves (the attack was ordered in four waves) was in possession of the first of the German trenches. This trench, which ran (as will be seen by the map) close along our whole attacking front, was not very strongly held, and the resistance offered by its defenders was no more than enough to warm our men up for what was to follow.

From this point it is necessary to trace the progress of the battle Brigade by Brigade rather than as a whole, for the problems confronting the 4th Brigade, on the right (as will be seen from the map), were different from those which the 6th Brigade, on the left, had to deal with. Suffice it to say here, by way of clamping the two sections of the movement together, that by 8 o'clock both Brigades were receiving the congratulations of the Divisional Commander, General Turner, upon their swift success. By 8.30 the last of our objectives was completely in our hands and being consolidated, while the enemy, dazed by the swiftness of their overthrow and demoralised to the point of panic by the implacable onslaught of the Tanks, had fled behind the inner defences of Courcelette. The way into the stronghold lay wide open.

The waves of an attack, under the latest conditions of warfare, go forward not in one long sweep, but in a succession of short advances strictly regulated by the successive steps of the barrage fire. Each time the barrage lifts forward—which it does according to a scheme previously worked out to the minute and the yard—the attacking lines must instantly move up behind it, as close as possible to the shelter of the appalling curtain of flame and death which it lets down before them. The progress of the wave being thus so strictly scheduled, it must often leave small enemy posts in its rear, or dug-outs sheltering furtive bands of machine-gunners. To deal with these "remainders"—which might easily become a serious menace, or even bring about complete disaster—behind the waves come the "mopping-up" parties, whose job it is to ferret out the hidden posts, clear the dug-outs, and gather in prisoners. The advance of the 4th Brigade on all its fronts, and in spite of desperate opposition, was so rapid and irresistible that it left behind plenty of work for its mopping-up parties.

Within fifteen minutes of going over the Brigade was in possession of another line of German trench, from three to four hundred yards behind the first line, running south-east from the Bapaume Road towards the Martinpuich Road. In the deep bays of this trench the contention was bitter and severe, and here occurred one of those instances of treachery for which the German has shown such peculiar aptitude. A party of the enemy threw up their hands, with, the customary cry of "Kamerad! Kamerad!" and surrendered to a company of the 18th Battalion, under the command of Captain S. Loghrin. As Captain Loghrin was accepting their surrender one of the party threw a bomb at him and blew him to pieces. The Captain's followers flung themselves forward in a fury, and not one German in that sector of the trench escaped the steel.

Throughout the advance the three assaulting Battalions of the Brigade, in spite of varying obstacles, succeeded in maintaining an even frontage. When the 18th, on the right, and the 20th, in the centre, fighting their way forward through the storm of shell and shrapnel and the deadly sleet of the machine-guns, had reached and taken Candy Trench, the final objective set them, it was still scarcely more than 7 o'clock. Three or four minutes in advance of them the 21st Battalion on the left, had reached the Sugar Factory and gained a footing there.

The Factory, though a redoubtable stronghold, had already been badly knocked about by our big guns. Now, within a very few minutes, it was surrounded on three sides by our exultant troops, who were not to be denied. After a mad half-hour of hand-to-hand struggle in a hell of grenade and machine-gun fire, from the dreadful turmoil of grunting, cursing, and shouting, the blood and the sweat of savage bodily combat, victory suddenly emerged, and the heap of ruins remained securely in our hands—along with 125 prisoners, of whom 10 were officers. One of the companies which distinguished themselves in this Homeric bout—"B" Company of the 21st Battalion—was commanded and most efficiently handled throughout the crisis of the affair by its senior non-commissioned officer, Sergeant-Major Dear, every one of its officers having fallen during its hard-fought advance along the Bapaume Road.

The unexpectedly swift collapse of this stronghold of the Sugar Factory—which the enemy had thought to make impregnable—was hastened, no doubt, by the intervention of one of the "Tanks." This monster, apparently eyeless, its carapace a daub of uncouth colours, squat and portentous as one of those colossal saurians which we picture emerging from the Eocene slime, had wallowed its slow, irresistible way up over the trenches and shell-holes, belching fire from its sides and its dreadful, blind, blunt snout. Bullets and shrapnel fell harmlessly as snowflakes upon its impervious shell. Bombs exploded thickly upon it, and, though wrapping it in flame, did no more than deface the fantastic patterns of its paint. Its path, wherever it moved, was spread with panic. In the teeth of the most concentrated fire it waddled deliberately up to the barriers of the Sugar Factory, trod them down without haste or effort, and exterminated a defending machine-gun with its crew. Then, crashing ponderously through or over every kind of obstacle, made a slow circuit of the Factory, halting stolidly here and there to blot out a troublesome nest of machine-gunners or to preside over the submission of a bunch of horror-stricken Huns. Its work done at this point, it lumbered off to seek adventure elsewhere, its grotesque—and, unfortunately, vulnerable—little tail bobbing absurdly over the shell-holes.

The 4th Brigade, having gained all its objectives, was now in no mood to rest content. The task of consolidation being well in hand, the 20th Battalion, in the centre of the line, sent forward a patrol under Captain Heron, M.C., the Battalion scouting officer. With great audacity and skill, Captain Heron worked his way along parallel to the Bapaume Road for a distance of 800 yards, and broke into the trench known as Gun Pit Trench. This was an important work, protecting, and in part coinciding with, the sunken road which forms the link between Courcelette and Martinpuich. Greatly daring—and profiting, no doubt, by the demoralising effect of the Tank's peregrinations in the neighbourhood—the little party bombed several dug-outs, and returned with two captured machine-guns and two prisoners to show for their splendidly insolent exploit. They reported the trench lightly held, whereupon the Brigade, promptly grasping the occasion, swept forward in a new—and thoroughly impromptu attack. Before 10 o'clock the trench was in our hands, with 50 prisoners (including two officers), a machine-gun, and three trench-mortars. Still unwearied, still unsated with success, the exultant Battalions pushed on and gained a line along the eastern side of the sunken road, where by 1 o'clock they had securely dug themselves in. This handsome and unpremeditated gain greatly simplified the consolidating of our position at Candy Trench and the Sugar Factory, and immediately made practicable the main operation against Courcelette itself.

With no less brilliancy and determination, meanwhile, the 6th Brigade, on the left, had been carrying out its share of the enterprise. From the first of the attack, or at least from its first objective (the first German trench) onward, it encountered a more stubborn resistance than that with which the 4th had to contend. Diagonally across the path of their advance, from the point on the right where the first German trench joined the Bapaume Road northwards to a juncture with McDonnell Road on the westernmost edge of Courcelette, ran a sunken road which had been strengthened by deep entrenching. It is shown on the map as Taffy Trench—and was so named by the troops doubtless in recognition of its complete harmony with the system of Sugar Trench, Candy Trench, and the Sugar Factory fitly presiding over all. Furthermore, the Brigade's advance was flanked throughout by strong enemy posts strung along McDonnell Road. The Battalion on the left (the 31st of Alberta) had not only to reduce these as it went, and to accomplish the reduction rapidly so as not to delay the main advance, but it had also to establish a defensive flank at the same time and thoroughly secure it in order to cover the advance against an enfilading assault from the network of German trenches spreading towards the north and north-west.

The attacking line of the 6th Brigade was somewhat differently organised from that of the 4th. Instead of being divided into three sectors, one for each of the three Battalions involved, it was divided into two sectors only. The 27th Battalion formed the attacking waves on the right half of the line, the 28th took the left half, while the 31st supplied the "mopping-up" parties to both sectors. The frontage allotted to the Brigade was about 1,800 yards, and the extreme depth of its attack, from the jumping-off trenches to the farthest objective, was something over a mile.

As with the 4th Brigade, the first objective (the original German front line) was carried swiftly and with little difficulty, and the whole line swept forward behind our barrage as coolly and according to book as if on the parade-ground. The German fire, both artillery and machine-gun, was fierce and effective, but as our bayonets came through it the enemy, as a rule, either fled, or threw up their hands, or scurried like rabbits into the dug-outs, refusing to face the cold steel. But on the left the wave of the 28th Battalion presently encountered a rock of sterner substance in the form of a machine-gun stronghold which had survived unscathed both our preliminary bombardment and our barrage. The little garrison here fought stubbornly in the effort to stay our onrush. The heart of their defence was an officer who both fought and directed magnificently and inspired his followers with his own courage. Our line was in some danger of being dislocated. As Canadian river-men would say, it had run up against a "snag" at this point. But one of our officers, Captain Bredin, of the 28th. perceiving a worthy foeman, ran out of the line and around the flank, and engaged him with a revolver. The German fell, and with his fall the spirit went out of his followers. The post was carried almost at once. Among the prisoners taken was a machine-gunner who was chained to his gun. It was a strange enough sight to our men, this highly-trained soldier fettered to his duty like a criminal, a steel stake driven into the ground on either side of him, one chain around his waist and another locked to an iron ring on his leg. The psychology of a race which discerns in such treatment an incentive to heroic endeavour is not unlikely to elude our apprehension.

By this time the German guns had realised the formidable nature of our advance and the depth of our penetration into the outer defences of Courcelette. The storm of shell and shrapnel that swept our line suddenly redoubled its fury. But our men went straight on through it, ignoring their casualties. The deadly diagonal of the sunken road was crowded with German troops, but our men flung themselves into it with the bayonet, and left it packed with German dead.

The course of this savage hand-to-hand struggle was thronged with incidents of individual heroism, so numerous as to make even a partial chronicling of them impossible in these pages. A couple of instances, however, may be cited as showing that the huge development of the mechanical element in modern warfare has not robbed the personal element of its opportunity or of its decisive influence. The case of Private Stevens, of the 28th Battalion, is one in point. His story may be quoted as follows from the Brigade Report:—"Just prior to the assault a party of six snipers from the 28th Battalion was posted in the shallow jumping-off trench to keep busy an enemy detachment of about 20 men which had been troubling our lines. All the members of this small party, except Private Stevens, were either killed or wounded, and Stevens himself had two holes through his steel helmet, a deep wound in his left shoulder, and a gash in his forehead. Nothing daunted, he kept on sniping and killed several of the enemy. His rifle was smashed by a shell just as the assault went forward. He picked up a rifle with fixed bayonet, and, dashing forward with the assault, entered an enemy's strong point, and single-handed captured five Boches and brought them back to our lines." The exploit of Lieutenant Clarkson, of the 27th Battalion, is, in another fashion, equally significant by reason of the unquenchable dominance of spirit which it displays. To quote again from the same Report:—"Lieutenant Clarkson was severely wounded in the knee, at the sunken road, and just as he fell four Germans came out of a deep dug-out. He at once covered them with his revolver, and, ordering them to improvise a stretcher out of a couple of rifles, made them carry him to our lines, and there handed them over prisoners. On the way in, as soon as his bearers showed the least sign of any opposition to his wishes, he quelled it with his revolver."

By a quarter to eight, in spite of all opposition and an unexpected addition to its task, the Brigade had gained its final objective and set itself strenuously to the work of consolidation, anticipating energetic counter-attacks. The addition referred to was an enforced extension to the left of about three hundred and fifty yards, which was found necessary in order to secure the flank. This operation, which was stubbornly resisted by strong German detachments in the Courcelette Road, was carried out with a rush by the 28th Battalion. Immediately the new line was secured three patrols were sent out beyond the line by the 31st Battalion. These patrols succeeded in establishing themselves, for purposes of observation, close to the southern edge of the village, and several of their scouts made their way into the village itself. The reports which they brought back were so sanguine that the Brigade, its blood being up, begged permission to pursue its success by an immediate assault upon the village. This proposal, however, was promptly vetoed, the Higher Command having already in view the plans for the afternoon. The impetuous 6th was obliged, therefore, to content itself with its very handsome achievement, which was not only so brilliant in itself as to deserve far more attention than it has received, but was also of vital importance to the unfolding of our final operations against Courcelette. The great advance of the 5th Brigade in the afternoon, with its swift success in bringing the whole village permanently within our lines, was a more outstanding exploit by reason of the conspicuousness of the goal gained thereby. But it must not be forgotten that Courcelette was fully half-won by the victories of the 4th and 6th Brigades in the early morning. The honours of the 2nd Division are fairly shared among all three Brigades. It was wholly because the morning triumph of the 4th and 6th Brigades went well beyond the utmost that had been expected of it that the afternoon attack was undertaken—and that September 15th became, in the Canadian War Calendar, COURCELETTE DAY.

CHAPTER V

COURCELETTE (CONTINUED)

The afternoon battle, which gave Courcelette solidly into our hands, was, as we have seen, the affair of the 5th Brigade, under Brigadier-General A. H. McDonnell, C.M.G., D.S.O. All the morning, fired by the successes of the 4th and 6th, the Brigade, held in reserve, had been fretting on the curb. As the G.O.C., with his Battalion Commanders, watched the fierce fighting and exultant progress of the other two Brigades, they began to wonder uneasily if the *rôle* of spectator was the only one that would fall to them in this great adventure. All doubts, however, were presently removed. At 3.30 came orders for the Brigade to take the village of Courcelette that same afternoon.

It was what in commercial terms would be called a "rush order," but the Brigade, already strung up to the highest pitch of expectancy, had no hesitation in undertaking to fill it. Operation orders were drawn up in haste; but that there was no sacrifice of explicitness and detail, on account of this haste, was proved by the accuracy and smoothness with which they worked out in the application. Officers and N.C.O.'s had to be instructed in their parts, yet all was so expeditiously managed that by 5 o'clock the advance, starting from its rendezvous point, was working its way up across the open under heavy shell-fire to the positions captured in the morning. It was from these new positions that the assault was to begin.

The three Battalions which made the attack—the three which actually carried out the storming of Courcelette—were the 22nd (French-Canadians, of Montreal), the 25th (Nova Scotia), and the 26th (New Brunswick). The 24th Battalion (Victoria Rifles of Canada) was held in reserve. The right of the attacking line was allotted to the French-Canadians, whose objective was the whole of the village to the right of the main street, running north. The left of the line was taken by the Nova Scotians, whose task was to storm the left half of the village. The steeple of the village church formed the landmark dividing the two objectives. The New Brunswickers followed close behind to support the assault, to deal with strong points which had proved too obdurate for the attacking waves, and thoroughly to mop up the whole village.

The action being a direct frontal attack, with no feints or flank diversions, and carried to its triumphant conclusion along its whole front, on schedule time and in precise accord with orders, the story of it does not afford that intense dramatic interest, those soul-racking fluctuations, those moments of terrible suspense, those snatchings of victory out of defeat, which may be found in the accounts of many lesser engagements. There were practically no fluctuations; and there was never, in the assailing waves, a moment of doubt as to the result. From flank to flank the advance was so irresistible, so implacable and undeviating, that within one hour and a quarter from the first lift of our barrage, the report went back to Headquarters that Courcelette was completely in our hands and that the work of consolidation was under way. Considering the distance and nature of the ground fought over and the tremendous obstacles to be overcome, it is obvious that there was no time for varying fortunes. By the very perfection and glory of the achievement the story of it must suffer.

Envisaged as a whole, the action may best be presented as the steady onflow of our waves close behind the successive lifts of our barrage. The movement was as deliberate and as strictly co-ordinated as if it were being executed on the parade-ground; for the enemy's fury of shell and machine-guns, though it could slash gaps in our lines, could not either check or hurry their inexorable march. Now here, now there, the lines would break into a little seething vortex of body-to-body struggle as they swept around and engulfed some rock of obstinate resistance. But for the most part these stubborn points were left to the uncompromising attention of the New Brunswickers, whose "mopping up" was thorough; and, having confidence in that thoroughness, the attacking lines refused to be delayed, but bombed and bayoneted their way straight on to their final objective. They gained it, and the most furious counter-attacks which an able and hardy enemy could afterwards hurl against it never availed to shake their grip upon it.

To grasp the details of the action it is necessary to follow the fortunes of the attacking Battalions individually. The total depth covered in the advance, as we have seen, was about 3,000 yards, and every yard of it under heavy shelling. The 22nd Battalion, on the right, led by Lieutenant-Colonel Tremblay, the Battalion Commander, in person, negotiated this portion of the advance in extended order at three paces interval (that is, in non-technical language, in an open line with a space of three yards between man and man). The two leading companies in this formation occupied a front of about 900 yards. One hundred and fifty yards behind them, in the same formation, came the other two companies of the Battalion. Two hundred yards behind them, again, came two companies of the 26th Battalion, also in two lines, to do the mopping up for their predecessors.

This first thin line, looking frail and inadequate indeed for the great task before it, moved on through the storm of death as steadily as if upon manoeuvres. But even upon manoeuvres it is difficult enough for a line so extended to maintain formation and direction. Now, with great gaps blown in it here and there, and each individual compelled to thread his way between endless shell-holes, some old and cold, some still smoking with poison fumes, the line took ground insensibly to the right and fell off toward Martinpuich. Its left was losing touch with the 25th Battalion across the Bapaume Road. Colonel Tremblay, perceiving the error in time, doubled across the whole front, swung up the right flank, and got the line once more facing its true objective. Three times he was thrown down and half-buried by shells exploding near him, but impatiently recovering himself he continued to guide the attack. The Battalion swept over the heads of the surprised

4th Brigade in Candy Trench, and then, pivoting on the Sugar Refinery, whirled to the left till its right rested on Gun Pit Trench. Fronting now due north, with shouts and cheers and shrill cries of exultation the excited French-Canadians stormed forward into Courcelette.

In their eagerness, these dark little men from the docks of Montreal were hardly to be restrained. They entered the outskirts of the village fairly on the heels of their own barrage, and suffered some loss from it before it lifted forward. The platoons of their extreme right ran into a torrent of machine-gun fire, which took heavy toll of them. But as soon these guns were located the little men were on to them like wild-cats, and from that quarter there was no further trouble.

The progress of the Battalion through the village was, in the main, one irresistible rush, scarcely delayed by the savage hand-to-hand encounters which developed all along its progress. Here and there a party of two or three would delay, perforce, to unearth and destroy a dangerous sniper's post or to bomb a threatening dug-out. But for the most part the front waves passed straight on, their left bounded by the main street running north, their right by the trenches outside the sunken road which forms the eastern limit of the village. They were not in the mood for stopping to take prisoners in their haste, but they gathered in about 300, unwounded, as they went. By 6.45 they had pushed clean through the maze of houses and established their lines clear beyond the Stone Quarry, which occupies the extreme north-eastern apex of Courcelette. They had utterly overthrown, destroyed, or captured a garrisoning force numerically superior to themselves and holding all the advantages of position and preparation.

This kind of fighting, this battling through the maze of half-ruined cottages, wrecked gardens, and tumbled walls was exactly to the taste of these eager and wiry Montreal Frenchmen. The variety of it, the scope it offered to individual adventure, appealed to them. Into such individual adventure they threw themselves with zest. A fiery sergeant, having captured a store of German bombs, loaded himself with them and set out to put them to the best possible use. He bombed a dug-out crowded with Huns. He rushed on to another and cleaned it up with equal effectiveness. He then, still single-handed attacked a third, but was shot down before he could throw his bomb. In spite of the heavy casualties which they suffered from beginning to end of their advance, the French-Canadians carried it through at a pitch of enthusiasm which made devotion easy and sacrifice of no account. But having thus gained their prize, the holding of it was presently to prove a more searching test of their quality. Throughout the next forty-eight hours they were to show, under terrible trial, as we shall see, a tenacity, an endurance, and a toughness of fibre no less admirable than the fire and *élan* of their attack.

Meanwhile, how had it been faring with the 25th Battalion, the men of Nova Scotia, on the left? The objective set them, it will be remembered, was that portion of Courcelette—the larger portion, as will be seen by reference to the map—which lay west of the principal street running north and south. Courcelette at this time, though much damaged, was still recognisable as a village. There were still streets to fight through, still houses and walls to serve as ambush for machine-gun or sniper. And the village church in the main street still stood, still held aloft its ancient spire, which was the landmark to guide the right flank of the Nova Scotians' line. It was the ceaseless—and futile—German bombardment of the place, after it had passed once for all into our hands, which pounded Courcelette into the dust and made of her one stony desolation with Pozières, Ovillers, and La Boiselle.

The first wave of the 25th Battalion was led by its commanding officer, Lieutenant-Colonel E. Hilliam. It was made up of "D" and "A" companies, led by their respective company commanders, Major Brooks and Major Tupper. And it occupied, in extended order, a frontage of about half a mile. For the work before it this line was daringly thin, but the coolness and steadiness of these Nova Scotian men fully justified the confidence of their leader, and the wide extension of the line kept down the casualties in passing through the heavy German barrage. In spite of this furious shelling; and the tortured ground to be traversed (which was nothing more than a jumble of shell-holes), this difficult formation was preserved as methodically as it on inspection parade, the whole battalion responding to its leader as a well-tuned machine responds to the touch of the operator.

At a distance of 600 yards from the village the advance came under very heavy machine-gun fire, and Major Brooks, who was leading D Company, the left half of the line, was killed, as was also Captain Dickey, the Adjutant, who accompanied Colonel Hilliam. Through this destructive fire the line swept on unwavering, without either delay or haste, to within 200 yards of the first houses. It was from among these houses that the stream of leaden death was issuing. Colonel Hilliam gave the word to charge, and the position—consisting of the whole southern outskirts of the village from the main street on the right, to the sunken road on the left—was captured with a rush. In this rush one of the enemy's machine-guns was taken, but the rest were successfully carried off by the survivors of their crews into the more northerly portion of the village.

The Nova Scotians were now somewhat ahead of their scheduled time—so much so, indeed, that they were beginning to get peppered with fragments from their own barrage. Colonel Hilliam, therefore, halted them, under cover of the cottages and garden walls, to take breath for the next thrust. He moved through the ranks, talking to each man personally, and found that, in spite of their casualties, they had small need of cheering or encouragement. Amid toppling walls and hurtling death and a pandemonium that no words can describe, they were smoking and chaffing as if their halt was a mere route-march rest along a peaceful roadside. But under this gay and laughing surface was the thrill of a fierce exultation, and, in the words of their commander, they were "like hounds straining on the leash" for the renewal of the attack. A few minutes more and the barrage lifted. The leash was loosed. The front line burst forward, and, bearing down all opposition in its rush, swept straight through to its objective, 300 yards beyond the northern boundary of the village. Here they at once began to dig in, and so judicious was the siting of their trenches that the enemy's artillery did not succeed in locating them till the next day. Colonel Hilliam, though wounded, remained on duty, personally supervising the task of consolidation. The second line, some fifty yards behind, came on more deliberately, finishing what its predecessor had left half-done, and taking up its position in support of the first. Numbers of the enemy were seen fleeing wildly up the slope and over the crest of the ridge beyond the village. They were pursued at once by the deadly individual fire of our sharpshooters and by the collective fire of certain sections working as fire-units as deliberately as if at range practice Though bomb and bayonet had been their chief weapons of late, the men had not forgotten the fine points of their musketry, and it was but a thin remnant of the fugitives that escaped over the ridge. These sons of Nova Scotia had proved themselves to be of the same indomitable temper as their forbears in "the land of the glens and the mountains and the heroes." They had displayed that blend of cold resolution and fighting fire which we associate with such storied Scottish regiments as the Gordons and the Black Watch.

Ten minutes later the Montreal men, enveloping the Stone Quarry, had joined up on the right. This was at 7 o'clock in the evening of the 15th. The whole of Courcelette was in our hands, and our grip was locked upon it, never to be shaken loose.

CHAPTER VI

HOLDING THE NEW GROUND

Meanwhile, the 26th Battalion, the men of New Brunswick, under Lieutenant-Colonel A. E. G. McKenzie, though denied the exultation of the first irresistible onward sweep to victory, were none the less getting their fill of hard fighting and contributing their full share to the splendid achievement of the day. They came in for sharp punishment, too in passing through the barrage which the enemy had promptly put up for the purpose of walling off the assault from its support. And the task which had been set them, of "mopping up" behind the assaulting waves proved to be a long, strenuous, and costly one. As the first waves of our attack raged across the village, numbers of the enemy flung away their rifles in panic, shouted the customary Kamerad! Kamerad!" and held up their hands in surrender. They were spared, and ordered to go back behind the lines. But after the wave had passed on, many of these, though essentially prisoners on parole, picked up their rifles again and fell to sniping our troops in the rear from convenient hiding-places in the gardens and cellars. When the New Brunswickers came along these traitors usually put up a desperate fight, having little reason to expect further mercy. The New Brunswickers, however, in spite of their many casualties, were in a triumphant mood and not inclined to inquire too closely into the deserts of their captives; and those who made haste to surrender again got the benefit of the doubt. All this business of "mopping up" gave opportunity for individual prowess, and the woodsmen and river-men, small farmers and independent townsmen of the sturdy Loyalist province threw themselves into it with peculiar zeal. By nightfall their task was nominally complete, and Colonel McKenzie was able to throw two of his companies into the trenches on the right of Courcelette in support of the 22nd Battalion, while the other two companies he posted on the left to support the 25th. But during all that night and the greater part of the following day he had small parties out scouring the ruins and the cellars, unearthing fresh dug-outs and discovering craftily-hidden sniping-posts. The Battalion suffered in all about 300 casualties, of whom 11 were officers. But the casualties which they inflicted upon the enemy, chiefly in their fierce bombing and bayonet work, were very heavy, and of unwounded prisoners alone they took just over 600, making a sufficiently handsome balance to their credit. General McDonnell, in a letter to Colonel McKenzie immediately after the relief of the Battalion, wrote: "New Brunswick may justly be thrilled with pride at the deeds done by her lads in this particular fight."

As the 25th Battalion had taken about 300 prisoners, and the 22nd approximately the same number, during their final sweep through the village, the total of prisoners to the credit of the 5th Brigade in this brief and brilliant action amounted to about 1,200, exclusive of the wounded. Among these prisoners were two colonels, one a regimental and the other a battalion commander. There was also substantial booty, including three 4.1 guns, seven machine-guns, seven trench-mortars, a locomotive and several railway trucks, with quantities of bombs, ammunition, and stores.

The village having thus been carried by storm, with such fine *élan* and disciplined valour, by the men of Nova Scotia, New Brunswick, and Quebec, the exultant victors had now an even sterner test to undergo. During three nights and two days they had to hold what they had gained against the most desperate efforts of a powerful and exasperated adversary to retake it. For this duty the 5th Brigade was reinforced by two additional Battalions, the 18th from the 4th Brigade and the 27th from the 6th; and General McDonnell was given command of the whole divisional front. On their right the 15th Division (Imperials), pounding their way onward through the twin village of Martinpuich, had kept an even front with the Canadian advance. But on their left the progress of the 3rd Division had been delayed by a formidable trench system known as the Fabeck Graben. The captured village, therefore, constituted the point of a dangerous wedge driven defiantly into the heart of the German position. It was not only a salient narrow and awkward, therefore, which General McDonnell, on this night of the triumphant September 15th, found himself called upon to consolidate and to hold, but it was one which both invited assault by its exposure and insistently challenged by its menace. Throughout the night, however, the enemy made no response to the challenge except by incessant shelling, their infantry, apparently, being for the time too much demoralised to face the conquerors again. By the afternoon of the 16th they had recovered, and being heavily reinforced, they made a desperate effort to recover their lost ground. From the trenches which they still held on the right of our position, by the cemetery, and from the direction of Destremont Farm, they launched no fewer than seven counterattacks upon the apex and the eastern side of the salient. This, as we have seen, was the frontage held by the French-Canadian Battalion, worn and weary, but elated by its dashing successes of the previous evening. Supported by a portion of the New Brunswick Battalion on their right, and by a strong advanced post from the Nova Scotian Battalion on their left front, the French-Canadians beat off all these assaults without yielding up a foot of their hard-won ground. In the meantime the Nova Scotians were dealing drastically with four counterattacks against their own front where they had hastily but thoroughly consolidated themselves along a line several hundred yards beyond the north-western outskirts of the village. It was during this consolidation that an adventurous Nova Scotian bomber—by name Private McIntyre—went scouting up a section of German trench, encountered a party of twelve Germans, coolly summoned them to surrender and marched them all in as prisoners. The results of these counter-attacks against the Nova Scotians were so unsatisfactory to the enemy that he did not repeat them, but turned his attention once more to the north-eastern face of the position, where the fact that he still held, with abundance of machine-guns, an obscure tangle of trenches between the Quarry and the Bapaume Road seemed to offer him better prospects of success. Here the 22nd Battalion, and the 26th, who had taken over the frontage between the Cemetery and the Bapaume Road to enable the diminished companies of the 22nd to shorten their line, on the nights of the 16th and 17th hurled back six more counter-attacks which were pressed with fierce determination. Upon the failure of these the Germans appeared sullenly to accept the loss of Courcelette, and confined themselves to harassing us with shell-fire and sniping. They found themselves fully occupied in blocking our ceaseless efforts to gnaw our way ever a little farther along the left of the road. On the afternoon of the 17th these efforts developed into a sharp attack by the 22nd and 24th Battalions upon that troublesome maze of trenches already referred to, just beyond the Cemetery. This attack was successful upon its left and centre, but was held up on its right by overwhelming machine-gun fire. It resulted, however, in a decided improvement of our position on the exposed eastern flank of the village.

While the 22nd and 24th Battalions were making this attempt on the right the Nova Scotians threw forward one company and a party of bombers on the left, endeavouring to seize a swell of ground just north of their lines. Though a minor attack, the men of Nova Scotia pressed it with great determination, their recent successes having rendered them unwilling to acknowledge that any obstacle could baulk them. This time, however, they found themselves held up, and were forced to draw back into their trenches after heavy casualties. Encouraged by this small flicker of success, the enemy sought to follow it up by a series of counter-attacks. As these grew more and more severe the reserve company of the New Brunswickers (the 26th Battalion) was thrown in to take a hand in the strenuous game. This went on throughout the night. Finally, during the progress of the heaviest counter-attack of all, a company of the 4th Battalion, 1st Brigade, came up to begin the relief; and the enemy was hurled back with severe punishment. On the morning of the 18th, the 2nd Division, battle-weary but triumphant and covered with distinction, was relieved, and drew off for a few days in rest camp at Rubempré; while the veteran 1st Division took over its proud lines on the left.

It is impossible to conclude the story of the winning of Courcelette without paying tribute to the heroic and extraordinarily efficient work of the Canadian Engineer and Pioneer companies throughout the whole course of the struggle. In consolidating our newly-won positions, in siting and digging communication trenches, in running up light railways to the new front, they laboured under the severe and incessant scouring of shell and machine-gun fire and endured heavy casualties without the stimulus of being able to strike back at their opponents. The daring and devotion of the Field Ambulance Service were such as to make all praise seem poor; and the deeds of heroic sacrifice in the rescue of the wounded were not less splendid than those enacted in the fighting itself. Among those who gave their lives in this noble work was the gallant officer directing it in the forward area, Lieutenant-Colonel R. P. Campbell, who fell in the hail of shrapnel. The arduous duties of carrying food and supplies for the fighting lines, throughout the engagement, were performed, at heavy cost, by the 24th Battalion, which thus contributed in fullest measure to the victory—and the casualty list—though deprived, except during the operation on the afternoon of the 17th, of its hoped-for share in the fighting. The gratitude of their fellow battalions, whose hands they so efficiently upheld, had to compensate them for their loss of the acclaim and exaltation of the great attack.

Of the 22 officers who went into the attack with the French-Canadian Battalion (the 22nd), 6 were killed and 11 wounded; and the Nova Scotian Battalion, by a curious coincidence, suffered the same number of casualties among its officers, viz., 5 killed, 8 wounded, and 4 missing—in all, 17 officer casualties for each of the two Battalions. With the 11 already noted in the 26th Battalion, 9 in the 24th,[1] 2 in the 5th Canadian Machine-Gun Company, 1 brigade bombing officer, and 1 O.C. Trench-Mortar Battery, we have a total of 58 officer casualties in the Brigade incurred during the actual operations of the 16th, 17th, and 18th. Of other ranks our casualties numbered 1,267.

[1] *Incurred during the perilous and essential duties of "carrying" for the Brigade throughout the whole operation.*

CHAPTER VII

MOUQUET FARM

Though it was to the 2nd Canadian Division the distinction fell of taking Courcelette, this signal triumph would not have been possible but for the simultaneous attacks of the 3rd Canadian Division on their left, across McDonnell Road. These attacks resulted, at the moment, in no great gain of ground, but they effectually held the attention of the Germans in the Fabeck Graben and Zollern Trench, and so protected the flank of the 2nd Division's advance. This, indeed, was all that it was intended to accomplish, the duty assigned to the 3rd Division in orders being merely to carry out such operations as might be necessary to protect the left flank of the main offensive. The task with which the Divisional Commander (Major-General L. J. Lipsett, C.M.G.) found himself confronted was an arduous one for he had peculiarly difficult ground before him, and such formidable defensive positions as Mouquet Farm and the Fabeck Graben and Zollern trenches; but it was accomplished with complete success, though not without heavy cost in casualties.

It was on September 7th that the 3rd Division moved south from Steenvoorde toward the region of the Somme, assembling in the neighbourhood of Cramont and Colon Villers. On the 10th they transferred to the Reserve area at Rubempré; and on the 12th they moved up into the fighting area, on the left of the 2nd Division, with headquarters at Usna Hill. On their left they had the 11th (Imperial) Division. The 8th Brigade (Brigadier-General J. H. Elmsley, D.S.O.) went first into the trenches, beyond the ruins of Pozières; while the 7th Brigade held itself in readiness at Vadincourt, and the 9th at Herissart. The Brigade was made up of the 1st, 2nd, 4th, and 5th Canadian Mounted Rifles. The 2nd and 4th Canadian Mounted Rifles were sent into the front trenches with the 1st in support at Chalk Pits, and 5th in reserve among the mounds of *débris* which had been La Boiselle. The task of taking over these front lines in the dark, by men totally unfamiliar with the lay of the land, over a wilderness of shell-holes and old, ruined trenches, where all landmarks had been obliterated, and through a hell of shrapnel, gas and high explosives, was in itself equivalent to a battle, and calculated to shake the morale of any troops but those of the finest nerve. It was accomplished not without loss, and vicissitude, and much thrilling adventure.

That same night of the 12th, hoping to profit by the confusion attending the taking over of the lines, the enemy launched a sudden attack from Mouquet Farm, upon the left sector of the divisional front, at the same time putting up a heavy barrage to prevent the supports from coming up from the Chalk Pits. The attack fell upon the 2nd Canadian Mounted Rifles (under Lieutenant-Colonel Bott), who now, after their fighting in the north, numbered only about 250 bayonets. It was a rude welcome to this fiercely contested line, where the struggle had been wavering back and forth for days; but the battalion was a seasoned one, and was not caught unready. With the aid of the Artillery and light trench mortars the assailants, after an obstinate effort, were beaten back with heavy loss.

On the evening of the 14th, the 1st and 5th Battalions of the Canadian Mounted Rifles were in the divisional front trenches (having relieved the 2nd and 4th Canadian Mounted Rifles), when the 11th Division, on our left, made an attack. The Germans retaliated by a counter-attack upon our sector. Our men had hot work for a time; and the help of the Canadian heavy guns was called in with effect. By half-past nine the attack had been beaten back, with much more loss to the enemy, on this occasion, than to ourselves.

On the 15th began the long series of gruelling struggles which, with varied fortunes and cruel losses, was to keep the 3rd Division under almost ceaseless strain throughout the next four weeks, until its withdrawal, with the 1st and 2nd Divisions, from the Somme area. According to the plan of operations for the great offensive on the 15th, the part assigned to the 3rd Division was, as has been noted, to form a protecting left flank to the offensive. This was to be effected by a thrust against the Fabeck Graben and Zollern trench systems; by running out a trench and establishing a strong post on the extreme right, so as to obtain an enfilading fire of machine-guns along the front of the 2nd Division's objective (thus taking a direct hand in the attack on Courcelette); and by raiding the trench system around that ancient thorn in our side, Mouquet Farm, with a view to lessening the German pressure further to the right. The duty of carrying out these operations was allotted to the 8th Brigade, which was already in occupation of our front lines west of McDonnell Road.

At 6.30 on the morning of the 15th the first move in the attack was made. The 5th Canadian Mounted Rifles (Lieutenant-Colonel Draper), on the right, rushed their first objective, the German front line, so swiftly that it was gained with few casualties. They jammed the enemy back up his communication trench some distance and established a block. Their gain was quickly consolidated and they set themselves to digging a new communication trench back to our lines. At the same time the 1st Canadian Mounted Rifles (Lieutenant-Colonel Andross), on the left, sprung their raid on Mouquet Farm. They gained entrance, after a brief resistance, and found the place full of German dead, the harvest of our barrage. Having hastily effected such damage as they could with the explosives at their disposal, they made their way back to their starting point, with one prisoner, having suffered only 25 casualties in the affair, which had lasted just about one hour. They had no sooner evacuated the farm than the German artillery came down upon it with a tornado of shells, which inflicted much more damage than our raiders had been able to accomplish.

So far all had gone well; and now news came across of the unexpectedly swift and brilliant success of the 4th and 6th Brigades in their attack on the approaches to Courcelette. Toward 10 o'clock it was decided, by telephone conference between General Byng and the Divisional Commander, that, as the 2nd Division was to proceed to the capture of Courcelette in the afternoon, the 3rd Division should simultaneously undertake a further advance, with the object of seizing, not only Fabeck Graben, but the crest of the low ridge beyond it. From this position, if they could attain it, they would not only support and protect the further advance of the 2nd Division on Courcelette, but overlook and threaten the formidable lines of Zollern Trench. For this venture the 8th Brigade shortened its line toward the left, and the 7th Brigade, hurrying up from Usna Hill, moved into the trenches on the right, forming contact with the left of the 2nd Division at Taffy Trench. The greater portion of the responsibility for the new attack thus devolved, very fittingly, upon the 7th Brigade, which came in fresh for the contest while the 8th had already been under three days and nights of trial. The interest of the story at this point, therefore, centres chiefly about the fortunes of the 7th Brigade under its able commander, Brigadier-General A. C. MacDonell, C.M.U., D.S.O.

The disposition of the Brigade for the attack was as follows: The right half of the attacking wave was taken by the "Princess Pats," under Lieutenant-Colonel Pelly, the left half by the 42nd Battalion (the 5th Royal Highlanders of Canada from Montreal), under Lieutenant-Colonel Cantlie. Immediately beyond the centre of the attacking line waited the 49th Battalion (the Edmonton Regiment, Lieutenant-Colonel Griesbach). The plan was for the 42nd and the "Princess Pats" to take the first two objectives and consolidate them. The 49th was then to pass on through to the third objective and dig in. Behind the 40th, again, stood the Royal Canadian Regiment, in support, under Lieutenant-Colonel C. H. Hill. The plan was well devised; but it was destined to encounter obstacles which prevented its complete accomplishment. In one vital respect, however, its purpose was fully attained. It gave the enemy all he could do on its front, thus perfectly, though at heavy cost, protecting the flank of the 2nd Division, and rendering possible the triumphant assault on Courcelette. The operation must, therefore, be accounted a complete victory for the 3rd Division, which thereby achieved what it was set to do in an entirely adequate manner, although not gaining all the ground which it had hoped to gain.

The task confronting the Brigade Commander at the very outset was a sufficiently hard one. He had to bring up his Brigade over five miles of extremely difficult and confusing ground, through a succession of destructive barrages, and deploy it for attack in broad daylight, in the very teeth of an enemy in force and furiously alert, along an almost shelterless frontage. This was accomplished on time, at 6 p.m. The attack was launched as planned, just at the moment when, to the right, the 5th Brigade was starting its final victorious advance on Courcelette. The men of the 42nd Battalion reached their first objective in fifteen minutes with comparatively light casualties; and by half-past six they had gained their portion of the second objective, the formidable Fabeck Graben. The "Princess Pats" meanwhile had carried their first objective with a rush; but running into a withering machine-gun fire on their right, they were partially baulked of their second objective. Only the two platoons of their left succeeded in getting into Fabeck Graben, where they established themselves in touch with the 42nd. On their right, for the next 200 yards or so, the trench was still held by the enemy in force. Beyond them again the trench was occupied almost up to the outskirts of Courcelette, by parties of the veteran battalion, which had burst their way, with magnificent audacity, through the hell of the machine-guns, and were holding on to the precarious gains with the tenacity of bulldogs. The heroism of these scattered groups was of incalculable service to the men of the 25th Battalion, then fighting their way through the western half of Courcelette.

Soon after 8 o'clock the 49th Battalion started up the sunken road on its way to attempt the third objective; and the Royal Canadian Regiment, supporting, took their places in the front line from which the attack had been launched. They got into Fabeck Graben, and held on there; but concentrated artillery fire and the massing of the Germans in Zollern Trench, and especially about its junction with the Fabeck Graben, made further progress for the moment impossible.

To the 8th Brigade, on the left, had been set but a single objective, namely, the more westerly sector of Fabeck Graben, running in the direction of Mouquet Farm. But one battalion, the 4th Canadian Mounted Rifles (from Eastern Canada, and commanded by Lieutenant-Colonel H. D. L. Gordon), was appointed to this operation. "B" and "C" Companies formed the attacking waves. But a heavy blow fell upon them at the outset, which, but for the ready initiative of the captain in command of "B" Company, would have upset the whole movement. "B" Company gained the jumping-off trench without mishap; but "C" Company, which was a little way behind, was caught fairly by the German barrage, just as it was deploying from the communication trench known as "Tom's Cut." The result was disastrous. Two of the platoons were practically wiped out. And the remaining two platoons were forced to draw back into the shelter of the trench. Perceiving that the whole operation of the Brigade was in jeopardy through this misfortune, the captain of "B" Company (Captain Coleman) came to a bold decision. Extending his company to occupy the whole frontage, he attacked at once, before the enemy became aware of their advantage. His thin wave made up for its deficiency in weight by the fury of its charge, burst into Fabeck Graben with bomb and bayonet, and carried the whole objective. Having secured his connection with the 7th Brigade on his right, he fought his way some distance along the trench to his left, and established a block to protect his heroic handful from interference from the direction of Mouquet Farm. It was an altogether notable feat, even among the many achievements of that memorable day. As soon as darkness fell, the remaining two platoons of "C" Company moved up into the captured position, a communication trench was dug back to our lines, and patrols were sent out toward Zollern Trench to guard against a surprise counter-attack. Throughout the affair the support of our artillery left nothing to be desired. Had it not been for the fulness and accuracy of our barrage the success of a single company extended over so wide a frontage would have been impossible.

Fabeck Graben having been thus secured by the 3rd Division, it was decided that the Division should, on the following day, the 16th, press on to the assault on Zollern Trench and the strongly defended position known as Zollern Redoubt, situated at a commanding cross-roads, about half a mile due north of Mouquet Farm, which had been giving us trouble for so long that it had acquired an evil fame out of all proportion to its importance. The ground about the farm was high, and peculiarly exposed to the enemy's fire from north, north-east and east alike, so that it was necessary to take not only the stronghold itself but the rolling ground far in advance of it, in order to be secure in its possession. All previous attacks upon it had been made from the south and south-east; but now the plan was to attack from the east. To this end it was absolutely essential that the eastern half of Zollern Trench should first be in our hands.

The whole operation, as will be obvious from a glance at the map, now depended on the gaining of our first objective, namely, the line of Zollern Trench east, as far west as Grandcourt Road. With that line in our possession, the way would be open to attack both Zollern Redoubt and Mouquet Far, with a reasonable chance of success.

The plan of operation was as follows: At 5 p.m. the 7th Brigade, which occupied the right of the line was to capture Zollern Trench and secure their hold upon it. Then, but not till then, the 9th Brigade (Brigadier-General F. W. Hill, D.S.O.) occupying the centre of the line, was to swing its right northward till it rested on Zollern Trench, and then move westward against Zollern Redoubt. This attack was not timed to start till 6.30, to allow for the completion of the movement of the 7th Brigade, upon which it hinged. The 8th Brigade, meanwhile, on the left, was to undertake the task of encircling Mouquet Farm on the east and north.

Throughout the afternoon all the proposed objectives were subjected to a heavy bombardment, which at 4.30 was intensified to a close barrage, behind the shelter of which the assaulting battalions of the 7th Brigade formed up for the attack. At 5 p.m. the first wave went over the top, the Royal Canadian Regiment on the right, the 42nd Battalion (Royal Highlanders, Montreal) on the left, with the 49th Battalion (Edmonton) in support.

The attack was ably planned and launched with the greatest resolution, but it met with an altogether unexpected weight and fury of opposition. It found the enemy massed before it in unprecedented force, and ran into a devastating storm of machine-gun fire from left and front. It turned out that the Germans had gathered all their available strength on that sector for an overwhelming counter-attack on Courcelette. The result was an unforeseen one for both sides, a stalemate as far as these operations were concerned. The great counter-attack, which might conceivably have wrenched Courcelette from the grasp of its weary conquerors, was shattered before it even got under way, and nothing was heard of it thereafter on any such scale. At the same time our attacking waves broke in vain upon the fiery parapets before them, and none gained an entrance to the trench.

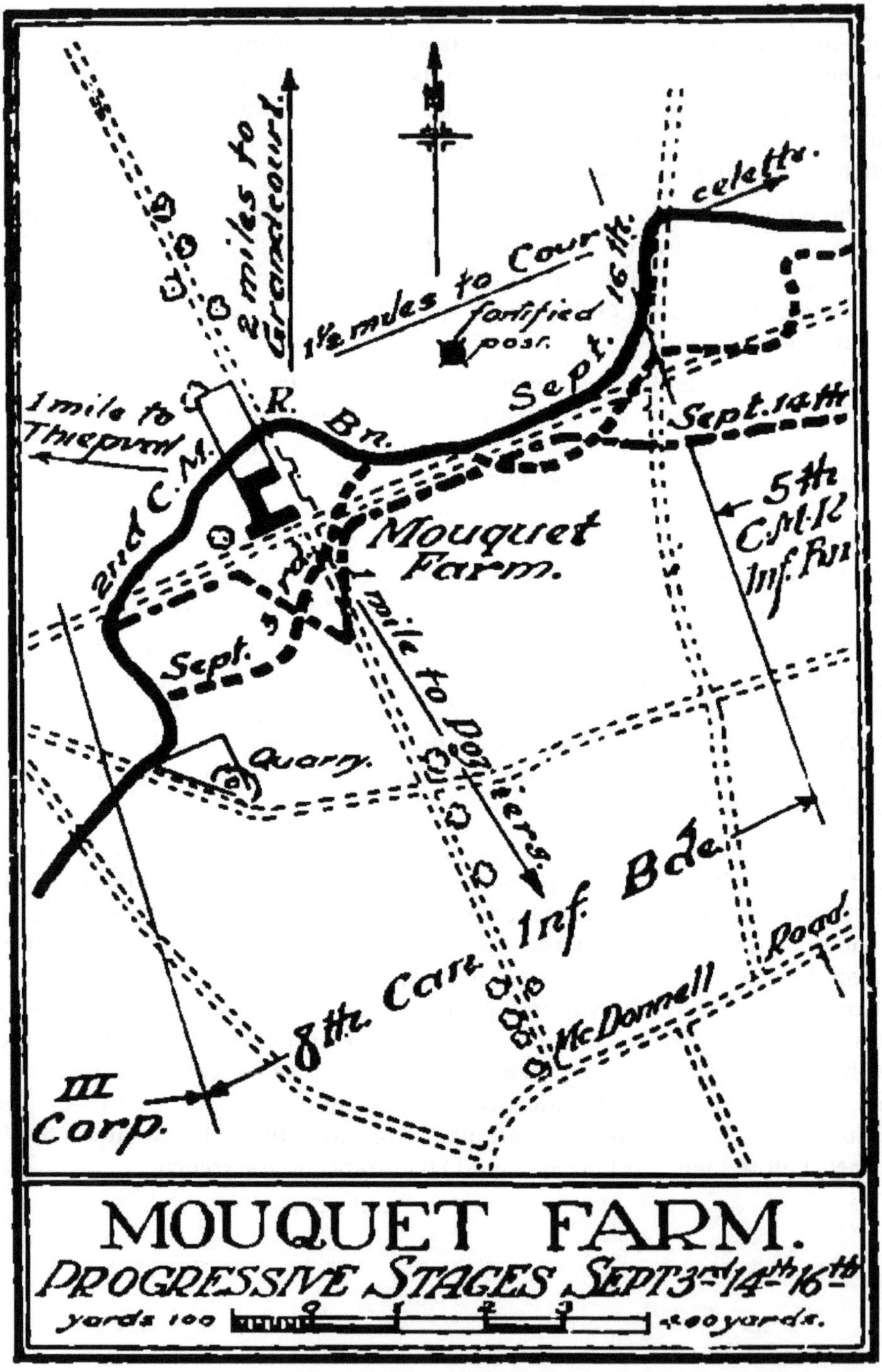

Map—Mouquet Farm. Progressive Stages, Sept. 3rd 14th 16th.

The 9th Brigade meanwhile had reached their jumping-off trench, and were waiting impatiently to move on Zollern Redoubt. The appointed hour went by; but the Zollern Trench was still in the enemy's hands, and they could not start. In this crisis the commander of the 7th Brigade ordered up his supporting battalion, the 49th, to add its weight to the attacking line. The enemy's barrages were so intense that the signal wires were all broken, and the order had to be sent through by runners. For these runners, too, as ill chance would have it, the barrages proved equally destructive, and the order never reached the 49th till 11 o'clock. By that time it was too late, and the order had been already cancelled. In the meantime, the leading battalion of the 9th Brigade had sent three platoons to the aid of the hard-pressed 42nd. General Hill had not yet given up hope of getting his blow in against the Zollern Redoubt and he asked that the artillery should keep up their barrage on the redoubt till 7.30, which was done. By this time, however, it was clear that the 7th Brigade had been baulked. Thus disorganised in its foundations the whole attack fell through and was abandoned, and our battalions, angry and bleeding, drew back into their own lines.

As far as the object with which it was undertaken is concerned, the operation was a confessed failure. But inasmuch as it brought to naught the great German counter-attack the failure was not without its compensations, and the account may be regarded as fairly squared. At the same time, while the major operation had thus missed its aim, a very important success had been scored for the Division by the 8th Brigade, on the extreme left. The 2nd Canadian Mounted Rifles, during the night of the 16th-17th, took Mouquet Farm. A party, under Major Foster, bombed the Germans out of a trench which covered the north side of the Farm, consolidated it, and established two machine-gun and bombing posts. Then other parties of the battalion entered the Farm itself, and blew up the dug-outs, wherein the garrison was sheltering. Among these dug-outs one was discovered which threw light upon the source of many past reverses. A cunningly concealed tunnel led northward from it to a maze of German trenches outside. By this tunnel, when Australians or Imperials had captured Mouquet Farm on previous occasions, the Germans had been wont to steal in with machine-guns and bombs and take them in the rear. Now, this tunnel was effectually closed by exploding a Stokes gun shell within it, and the enemy beyond were sealed away from further mischief.

In a few hours a new trench was dug, completely surrounding the Farm, and the stronghold so drenched with blood, so often won and lost again, so long a menace to our lines on the south and east, was at last securely in our hands. Before daylight the Canadian Mounted Rifles handed it over, with pardonable exultation, to a relieving Battalion of the 11th (Imperial) Division. On this day the 8th Brigade moved back to the Brickfields at Albert, and the 7th to Tara Hill; and the 9th Brigade took over their lines. The next few days were occupied with sharp but fluctuating struggles, carried out by the 1st Division on the right around Courcelette and the 3rd Division on the left, which yielded no permanent result except the improvement of our position between Courcelette and the Bapaume Road, and a slight but valuable gain of ground along the northern outskirts of the village, towards Kenora Trench. Zollern Graben still defied us. Though it was taken on the 20th, for an extent of 250 yards, by the 43rd (Cameron Highlanders of Canada, Winnipeg), and 58th (Toronto) Battalions, we were not yet able to maintain our hold upon it. These confusing and sanguinary struggles may be regarded as leading up to and preparing the way for the next great series of operations, which aimed at, and at last, after bitter cost, resulted in, the capture of Regina Trench.

CHAPTER VIII

REGINA

The two outstanding features of the Canadian Corps operations on the Somme in the late summer and autumn of 1916 are undoubtedly the capture of Courcelette and the grim struggle for Regina Trench, but nothing could be greater than the contrast between the two. Courcelette, as we have seen, was captured by a swift and sudden operation, perfectly planned and brilliantly executed—a clear-cut victory without flaw or hitch. On the other hand, the Canadians fought for over a month to obtain possession of Regina, attacking again and again according to carefully laid plans, sometimes to gain by sheer valour a temporary footing in the trench, only to be hurled back, fighting stubbornly, by overwhelming numbers; at other times to face unsuspected and murderous machine-gun fire which almost wiped the assaulting platoons out of existence. Yet each successive attack pushed won a little nearer to the goal, until at last, after a month and more of harassing vicissitudes, a final rush secured the victory.

Regina Trench first came within the scope of Canadian operations during the offensive of September 26th and 27th, when it was the ultimate objective of the attack. At no time, however, did the attacking troops get within striking distance of this last objective.

It was on October 1st that the first elaborate and comprehensive attack was made, in conjunction with the III Corps on the right and the II Corps on the left. The Canadian line at this date ran from the north-western corner of Destremont Farm in a general westerly direction, with a large loop to the north around the North Practice Trenches, to the junction of Grandcourt Road and the recently captured Hessian Trench. From this point the line followed Hessian Trench westward to the Corps boundary on the left, a short distance west of the junction with Courcelette Road. The task set the Corps was to occupy a line from the above-mentioned point at Destremont Farm north-westerly to the junction of Regina Trench and East Miraumont Road, thence along Regina to a road running north and south near the Corps' left boundary, where the line bent back sharply to the Hessian Trench line.

The portion of Regina Trench which lies to the east of the junction with East Miraumont Road was not included in the scheme of operations.

There were seven Battalions in the line of attack. These were, from right to left, the 20th and 18th of the 4th Brigade, the 22nd, 25th, and 24th of the 5th Brigade, and the 5th Canadian Mounted Rifles and the 4th Canadian Mounted Rifles of the 8th Brigade. Thus the 2nd Division, on the right, had five Battalions of two Brigades in the line, and the 3rd Division, on the left, had two Battalions of one Brigade taking part in the assault.

It will be as well, perhaps, to describe the general result of the action before attempting to follow the fortunes of each Battalion in detail. The greatest measure of success was attained on the right, where the line was advanced some 500 yards in such a manner that both flanks of the 4th Brigade line were brought up in line with the loop around the North Practice Trenches in the centre of the Brigade area. In the centre the 5th Brigade managed to maintain itself for a time in Regina Trench, but was afterwards forced to retire. It succeeded, however, in capturing and holding Kenora Trench up to within sixty yards of the junction with Regina, and held posts up Courcelette Trench and the West Miraumont Road about half-way between their attacking line and Regina. The Canadian Mounted Rifles of the 8th Brigade on the left also succeeded in reaching Regina at several points. Heavily counter-attacked, they managed to hold on for a considerable time, but in the end they were driven back to their starting line in the Hessian Trench.

At 3.15 p.m. on October 1st—a clear, bright day—the attack was launched. The 20th and 18th Battalions, on the right, advanced respectively 400 and 500 yards over the open. This brilliant feat, comparable to the famous advance over the open at Courcelette, was only rendered possible by the cover afforded by the shell-holes. In spite of severe machine-gun fire from the direction of Pys and Le Sars, the 20th had established themselves in their position, with their flanks formed, before their flanking battalions, the Imperial on the right and the 18th on the left, had come up. They had advanced to a point about 150 yards N.N.W. of their true objective, which would account for the fact that the 18th Battalion appeared to be behind them to the left. This was the situation on the morning of October 2nd.

Meanwhile, the 18th had advanced and dug in. Their left, however, was in a very critical position, for the 22nd Battalion—the right battalion of the 5th Brigade—had not come up. The French Canadians, assaulting with their usual dash and intrepidity, had encountered a withering machine-gun and rifle fire from the front and flanks. A few who reached Regina Trench were either killed or captured. A few wounded managed to return to our lines. So badly had the Battalion been cut up that the 26th (New Brunswickers), in close support, took over that part of the line.

The 25th Battalion (Nova Scotians), the centre battalion of the 5th Brigade, stormed Kenora Trench and moved on steadily towards Regina. Machine-gun fire from front and flanks took heavy toll of them, but those remaining reached the wire in front of Regina and started to dig in. A few odd parties actually succeeded in forcing their way into Regina. After fighting desperately for some time in an endeavour to connect up with the 24th on their left, they were nearly all killed or taken prisoners. A few managed to return wounded to the lines.

The right company of the 24th Battalion (Victoria Rifles of Canada) crossed Kenora Trench and entered Regina east of the junction of Kenora and Regina, and the centre and left companies succeeded in reaching their objective in Regina

Trench with their left on Twenty-three Road. They were separated from the 25th on their right by a strong enemy post, and on the left, owing to the repulse of the 5th Canadian Mounted Rifles, their flank was in the air. Furious fighting ensued in Regina Trench from Twenty-three Road to Kenora. "A" Company, which had entered Regina just east of the junction with Kenora, fought fiercely against superior numbers. Eventually what was left of them—for the majority were either killed or captured—retired foot by foot. Batmen, cooks, and servants were hurried up to help stem the overflowing tide of Germans. On the left the Battalion was pushed back from Twenty-three Road to a short distance from the junction of Kenora and Regina Trenches. Here a dogged stand was made. Meanwhile, a few small parties of the 24th and 25th, who were digging in in front of Regina, east of the trench junction, gradually retired to Kenora. The whole of Regina remained in the hands of the enemy with the exception of a post held by the 24th between the point where Kenora and Regina join and Twenty-three Road. During this struggle the 26th, holding the original line of the 22nd with the remnants of that Battalion, could spare very little in the way of reinforcements, only some fifty of all ranks being available.

In the meantime, the 8th Brigade, on the left, had been having a very rough time. From reports received very shortly before the attack took place it became evident that in many places the wire in front of Regina had not been thoroughly cut by the artillery. This was especially the case on the front assigned to the 4th Canadian Mounted Rifles, whose left attack had to be modified in consequence.

The Brigade attacked with the 5th Canadian Mounted Rifles on the right and the 4th Canadian Mounted Rifles on the left. The right of the right attacking company of the 5th Canadian Mounted Rifles was held up by wire and ran into terrific machine-gun fire. The left attack came under heavy fire about 50 yards from its objective, but as no further opposition was encountered, it effected a lodgment in Regina. Work was immediately started on the badly-damaged trench, and blocks were put in on the flanks. And not a moment too soon. Repeated counter-attacks were made, all of which were successfully repulsed, excellent use being made of a captured machine-gun.

The right company of the 4th Canadian Mounted Rifles' attack, with the exception of one platoon which was hung up by wire, apparently reached its objective, but heavy counter-attacks from the direction of the sunken road were too much for its depleted strength.

The left of the 4th Canadian Mounted Rifles was forced to modify its assault on account of the uncut wire. A very unusual scheme of attack was adopted. After moving down the communication trench the attackers deployed on the German side of the wire. Unfortunately, a heavy enfilading machine-gun fire from the north-east and north-west wrecked the attack. One platoon, immediately to the west, advancing with the greatest resolution, was almost wiped out, and a bombing party which succeeded in effecting an entry into Regina was at length forced to retire.

With the exception, therefore, of the successful advance of the 4th Brigade on the right, the situation during the afternoon was that at various points in Regina desperate hand-to-hand fighting was taking place.

At 6.30 p.m. the state of affairs was approximately as follows. The 4th Brigade was consolidating its position and attempting to gain touch with the 70th Brigade on the right. Parties of the 24th and 25th Battalions were in Regina Trench, fighting manfully against superior numbers and bombing towards each other against the enemy, who appeared to be in considerable strength at the junction of Kenora and Regina Trenches. Between the East and West Miraumont Roads the situation was obscure, as the result of the attack of the 22nd Battalion had not yet been accurately ascertained. They were thought to be in their objective, whereas, as we have seen, they encountered machine-gun and rifle fire of such intensity that success was out of the question. Yet they had managed to push the assault home, for about 50 men entered Regina and were only forced to retire after a short, sharp fight against overwhelming odds.

At the same time the left company of the 5th Canadian Mounted Rifles ("A" Company), reinforced by parties from "C" and "D" Companies, was fighting desperately to maintain its foothold in Regina. Repeated counter-attacks were heroically repulsed.

The situation was rapidly becoming clearer. Reinforcements were ordered to be sent up to all units which had succeeded in reaching their objectives. Bombing parties were to converge against the German parties in the trench, and every effort was made to improve and consolidate the positions won.

A determined attempt was made by the 5th Canadian Mounted Rifles in Regina to join up with the 24th on their right. One company of the 1st Canadian Mounted Rifles was placed at the disposal of the O.C. 5th Canadian Mounted Rifles for the purpose, and two platoons, with the 5th Canadian Mounted Rifles' bombers in front, pushed eastward along the trench to the point at which they expected to get into touch with the 24th. The trench they traversed was found to be exceptionally strong, seven feet deep, with twelve-foot dug-outs every second bay. It had not been damaged by artillery. On reaching their objective they perceived a large body of men ahead of them, which they naturally assumed to be the expected 24th Battalion party. Unfortunately, this was not the case; it was, in fact, a German counter-attack advancing in force. These Germans attacked and drove them back, foot by foot, to their starting point. A second attack was then organised, which again succeeded in penetrating to the objective point. This point, with the intervening stretch of trench, was stubbornly held throughout the night until 5 a.m. on the 2nd, when heavy counter-attacks pushed in both flanks and compelled the evacuation of the trench. Even then the forty or so survivors clung to a line of shell-holes south of the trench for some time before being forced to retire to Hessian Trench. From this time the 8th Brigade held the original line until it was handed over to the 7th Brigade on the night of October 2nd-3rd.

On the right the dawn of October 2nd revealed the situation to be approximately as follows. The 20th Battalion, with the flanks secured, was established, as has been described, about 150 yards N.N.W. of where they were supposed to be with the 18th Battalion consolidating on their left slightly to the rear. The British on the right (70th Brigade, 2nd Division, III Corps) had reached the southern position of the Le Sars line on the previous evening and were apprehensive as to their left flank. Patrols were sent out by both British and Canadians in an endeavour to establish contact; yet although they came into touch during the evening of the 1st, it was not until the evening of the 2nd that proper contact was effected and connecting posts planned.

The left flank of the 18th Battalion, left in the air owing to the failure of the 22nd to come up, was secured by the Battalion Lewis guns.

The parties of the 24th and 25th Battalions of the 5th Brigade[2] which had fought so strenuously in Regina were unable to maintain themselves in the trench as long as did the 5th Canadian Mounted Rifles on their left, but were driven out during the night.

The 6th Brigade, waiting to relieve the 5th, was finally ordered? in the very early hours of October 2nd, to take over the line as it stood—that is, the captured portion of Kenora Trench, the post in Courcelette Trench, and the new trenches to the west of Kenora.

This Brigade also took over the 4th Brigade line as far east as the Pys Road.

There were no fresh developments during the day. Every nerve was concentrated on strengthening and consolidating the positions won. The 20th Battalion had already a shallow trench dug across their whole front. The 18th likewise were consolidating their position. In the centre the 6th Brigade, similarly engaged, had a rather quiet day, and on the left the 8th Brigade, terribly depleted, was holding its original line in the Hessian Trench.

The Battalions of the 4th and 8th Brigades which had borne the brunt of the offensive were relieved as soon as possible—the 8th by the 7th on the night of October 2nd-3rd, and the 4th and 6th on the night of the 3rd by the 9th Brigade. The fresh Brigades were warned to prepare for a renewed offensive.

In spite of the wretched weather which now set in, there was no diminution

[2] The 5th Brigade began their tour in the line 1,717 strong (all ranks). Their casualties during the tour amounted to 944 all ranks, making their strength on coming out 773 all ranks.

In the 5th Brigade on October 2nd the 5th Canadian Mounted Rifles, with attached details, numbered only 250 effectives, and the 4th Canadian Mounted Rifles but 175.

The casualties of the Canadian Corps from September 27th to noon on October 4th were as follows:

OFFICERS.		OTHER RANKS.	
Killed	25	Killed	847
Wounded	89	Wounded	3,364
Missing	8	Missing	1,176
Total	122	Total	5,387

Grand total all ranks 5,509

in the active preparations for renewing the attack or in the ardour of the troops. Jumping-off trenches were constructed and orders were expected from day to day. Postponements, however, were inevitable. More time was required for adequate artillery preparation. Wire had to be cut and ammunition to be accumulated in the forward positions, which were now at a distance from any practicable roads. The attack eventually took place on October 8th.

In the interval the most noteworthy incident was the occupation of Kendal Trench on October 4th by the Royal Canadian Regiment, who succeeded in establishing a post within 25 yards of the enemy. One-third of this trench—nearest our lines—was found to be practically obliterated.

On October 8th the offensive on a large scale was resumed. In conjunction with the 23rd and 25th British Divisions, on the right and left respectively, the Canadian Corps attacked on a two-division frontage, the 1st Division being on the right and the 3rd on the left. Each Division had two Brigades in the line. The Battalions engaged, from right to left, were the 4th and 3rd of the 1st Brigade, the 16th and 13th of the 3rd Brigade, the 58th and 43rd of the 9th Brigade, and the Royal Canadian Rifles and 49th of the 7th Brigade.

The objective of the 1st Division was to depend upon the degree of success attending the preliminary operation undertaken on the 7th by the 23rd Division. If this Division attained its second objective—i.e., the remainder of Le Sars Village with its left on the Chalk Pit—the 1st Division would attempt the whole objective assigned to it. In the event of partial failure on the part of the 23rd Division, the 1st Division would not attempt to carry the quadrilateral. The 23rd, however, were completely successful, and accordingly the objective of the 1st Division became as outlined below.

The 1st Brigade, on the right, was to capture and hold a line running approximately north-west from a point in Below Support Trench just west of the Dyke Road to the junction with Gallwitz Support Trench, thence south-west to the junction of Regina and Farmer's Road. At this point the objective of the 3rd Brigade began. It followed Regina Trench west as far as the point M.13.b.6.1 (see map).

To the left of this lay the portion of the objective allotted to the 9th and 7th Brigades of the 3rd Division. Of this the 9th Brigade was to attack and occupy the line of Regina from M.13.b.6.1 west to the junction with Pys Road, north-west to the German cross-trench between Courcelette Trench and West Miraumont Road, and then due west along this trench to, but not including, West Miraumont Road itself.

The 7th Brigade was to form a defensive flank from the junction of Twenty-three Road to West Miraumont Road down the latter to Regina Trench along the trench to the junction with the communication trench (see map), at which point the flank was turned back to Hessian Trench.

In the event of success the 7th Brigade was to push out from West Miraumont Road and establish a flank along Twenty-three Road after dark.

At 4.50 a.m. the long line of attack moved forward. The 4th Battalion, on the right, was held up by wire in front of the first Below Trench. Compelled to work round to the left, thereby rather crowding the 3rd Battalion, they entered the first, Below Trench just south of the quadrilateral and proceeded to bomb south of Dyke Road. Connection was established with the 23rd Division on the right and with the 3rd Battalion on the left. Owing to the greater resistance which the 4th Battalion encountered at first, their supply of bombs became exhausted in spite of gallant attempts to replenish it. In consequence, they were compelled to borrow some from the 3rd Battalion, which had had less resistance to overcome. This generosity on the part of the 3rd Battalion cost them dearly later on. Having also lent bombs to the 16th Battalion on their left, they found themselves, when heavily counter-attacked about 2.15 p.m., hopelessly short of munitions. The enemy attacked in great force and with great determination. They poured down the first and second Below and the first and second Gallwitz Trenches, rushed the three posts which had been established in the captured trenches, and drove a wedge through the quadrilateral, even coming over the open from the second Below Trench.

The situation of the 3rd and 4th Battalions was now extremely precarious. Attacked by a superior force and without an adequate supply of bombs, they fought tooth and nail to maintain their foothold. The S.O.S. signals failed. A wedge was driven between the two Battalions. The 3rd was bombed down Regina Trench with a few of the 4th, while the 4th was bombed down the first Below Trench.

On account of the congestion in Regina Trench which naturally resulted, a number of men of the 3rd Battalion occupied shell-holes in front of the trench, doing considerable execution with their rifles.

Lieutenant Chatterton behaved with the greatest gallantry. He got some of his men out on the north side of Regina Trench and attempted a bayonet charge. His charge was repulsed, and he himself was shot through the shoulder. Crawling back into the trench and tying up his arm in a sling, he rallied some men and got out on the south side of the trench. Another bayonet charge was attempted, in which the intrepid Lieutenant was killed. Major Haddon, Major Mowat, and Major Bennett led a similar charge, Major Mowat being killed. All attempts to stem the onrushing tide were unavailing. In the end about 100 men got back to the original line.

Meanwhile, the 4th Battalion was being bombed down the first Below Trench. For hours a desperate conflict raged in the trench. Whenever the 4th Battalion was able to borrow bombs from the 23rd Division on their right, they gained ground; whenever the supply of bombs ran low they were forced to give way. This give-and-take combat lasted until about 6 p.m., when the survivors, about 120 in number, dropped over into the Dyke Road in the 23rd Division lines.

The attack of the 3rd Brigade, on the left of the 1st, developed along very similar lines. Early reports were to the effect that the objectives had been gained by the 16th and 13th Battalions. "Everything looks very well" and "Situation well in hand," were the reports sent up to the Brigade. Soon, however, a more unfortunate state of affairs was revealed. The 16th Battalion, it appeared, had indeed reached its objective, but the left flank had been bombed cut. The remainder, on the right, fought for a long time with great stubbornness and tenacity. Lieutenant Hall sent in a message about 7.30 a.m. to say that, so far as he was aware, he was me only unwounded officer left.

The German counter-attack in the early afternoon which drove back the 3rd and 4th Battalions dashed itself in vain against the right flank of the 16th. The position of the Battalion was, nevertheless, far from secure. On the left the 13th Battalion had encountered heavy wire in front of the German trench. A few men of the Battalion apparently managed to get in with the 16th. The attack against a position strongly held and protected by impassable wire was necessarily doomed to failure, and a message from Major McCuaig, about 8 a.m., stated that the 13th had been compelled to retire. Their casualties were very heavy. They lay on the far side of the crest, in full view of the enemy, whose snipers cut off communication.

The left flank of the 16th was thus left in the air throughout the day. Their right flank was left exposed when the 1st Brigade was driven back in the afternoon. In this precarious situation they held on grimly, even though, owing to the exposed nature of the ground, snipers and machine-guns made it practically impossible to get a supply of bombs up, until, late in the evening, all possibility of success elsewhere having ceased to exist, they were ordered to abandon the position they had so stoutly held and to retire to their jumping-off trenches. The situation had to be accepted as it stood; the battalions were consolidated, removed as soon as possible in favour of the supporting battalions, and the line generally linked up and strengthened.

The ill-luck which had attended the assault of the two Brigades of the 1st Division also dogged the gallant efforts of the 9th and 7th Brigades of the 3rd Division.

During the few days' preliminary bombardment of the front-line wire, careful reconnaissances of the wire were made. Reports received just prior to the attack indicated that the wire in front of the objective had been well cut for the most part, and both Brigades expressed confidence on this point. But, as in the operations of October 1st, it was discovered later that a considerable amount of wire remained.

This fact materially affected the success of the operations. Yet the reports were not, on the whole, inaccurate, as on the night before the attack the Germans threw out large quantities of loose wire, which formed an awkward obstacle, and a second line of staked wire was encountered immediately in front of the trench at various points. Direct observation of this wire, particularly between Twenty-three Road and the junction of Regina and Kenora Trenches, had been particularly difficult and uncertain.

In spite of adverse weather conditions, jumping-off trenches were prepared along a large portion of the divisional front, and at 4.50 a.m., zero hour, the two Brigades advanced to the assault. A heavy rain, which commenced shortly afterwards and continued throughout the greater part of the day, contributed largely to the difficulties of the situation.

At zero hour the 9th and 7th Brigades moved forward with the rest of the long line of attack. From early reports, received from wounded men, it seemed that both Brigades had obtained their objectives. Unduly optimistic reports of this sort are easily explained. A wounded man sees his comrades advancing steadily within striking distance of the objective, and in perfect good-faith reports that apparently his unit has attained its objective. Appearances, however, were never more deceptive than in the present instance.

For some time after the attack began no definite news could be obtained about the 9th (right) Brigade. At 8.50 a.m. they reported that their left Battalion (the 43rd) had been held up by wire, and that only a portion of the right Battalion (the 58th) had effected a lodgment in Regina, from which they were later driven out. The left company and left half of the centre company of the 58th suffered severely before they reached Regina Trench. At the trench itself all three companies encountered heavy wire. The wire had been very little damaged by our artillery, and presented a formidable obstacle. Heavy machine-gun fire was brought to play upon the three companies in front of the wire.

The greater part of the right company were able to force an entry through a small sally port. Having gained a foothold in the trench, our men worked along to the right and held for about thirty minutes some 100 yards of the trench, up to a strong bombing post situated approximately on the right flank of the Battalion's objective.

The left portion of this company meanwhile entered Regina through another sally port, made their way as far as a communication trench on the left, and on the right established contact with the remainder of the company on the right.

All this time the centre and left companies were striving, heroically but unsuccessfully, to penetrate the wire. This left the right half of the Battalion, in Regina Trench, most precariously situated. Both flanks were in the air; on the right of the 58th the left Battalion (the 13th) of the 1st Division had been repulsed, and on the left the left section of the Battalion had failed. The Germans, taking immediate advantage of the opportunity, attacked right and left from the bombing post and communication trench already mentioned. After a fierce struggle the survivors of the 58th were expelled, and made their way, as best they could, back to their lines.

The 43rd Battalion, on the left of the 8th Brigade, also managed to establish themselves for a time in Regina Trench. Uncut wire effectually stopped the right and centre companies, even though a few individuals here and there succeeded in getting into the trench, never to return. But the left company, like the right of the 58th, got in. Some of them lost direction, and entered Regina with elements of the Royal Canadian Regiment on the western side of West Miraumont Road.

A counter-attack in overwhelming force followed almost immediately, and only about ten men of this company returned to our lines.

Meanwhile, on the left the 7th Brigade had also effected a lodgment in Regina. On the Brigade's right the Royal Canadian Regiment occupied Regina for a distance of 100 yards west of the West Miraumont Road. The enemy were still between them and the 49th on the left.

The 49th had also succeeded, according to reports, in pushing through to their objective. Two companies were reported to be at the junction of Kenora and Regina Trenches with some men of the Royal Canadian Regiment. They were bombing eastward in an endeavour to connect with the latter battalion. This was the situation at 7 a.m. As it appeared altogether likely that complete success would result if supports were brought up and the attack pushed resolutely home, the Princess Patricias, in support, were moved close up (two companies in the jumping-off trench and two in the Fabeck Graben), ready to advance whenever called upon.

On the Brigade right the Royal Canadian Regiment attempted to reinforce their troops in Regina by moving a company up the West Miramont Road. Heavy machine-gun fire foiled this attempt.

More definite information regarding the situation now began to come in. It was ascertained that the right and centre companies of the R.C.R. had entered the trench without serious casualties, but that the left company had been hung up by heavy machine-gun fire. The two companies which had entered Regina proceeded to mop up the numerous dug-outs in this portion of Regina and pushed out a strong patrol along the West Miraumont Road. A bombing party also bombed their way westward along Regina in an attempt to gain touch with the 49th, who were reported to have effected a lodgment to their left.

This report, however, was unduly optimistic. The right company of the 49th, bearing a trifle too far to the right, eventually reached Kenora Trench and occupied it under heavy fire. The centre and left companies, advancing straight on their objectives, passed through a row of well-cut wire, only to find further progress blocked by the presence of an unsuspected new row of wire, entirely undamaged. With dogged resolution they made their way along the front of the wire, seeking a gap. None was found, and after losing heavily they finally got into Kenora Trench. Animated by the most intense determination to reach their objective at all costs, they pushed three bombing parties up Kenora Trench. Every party met the same fate—wiped out by the Germans concentrated at the junction of Kenora and Regina Trenches.

The situation on the 3rd Divisional front at 9 a.m. was therefore as follows. On the right the 58th Battalion of the 9th Brigade, had effected a temporary lodgment from which they had shortly afterwards been expelled. The 43rd Battalion had failed to get in on the left, the R.C.R. had got in with two companies, but the 49th, on their left, reported successful at first, had failed to obtain any footing in the objective.

At this stage of the operations the Corps Commander visited the 3rd Divisional Headquarters. After studying the situation, he gave orders that every effort should be made to secure the portion of Regina Trench held by the 7th Brigade westward from the West Miraumont Road, and that, if necessary, supports and reserves were to be sent up to ensure success. With West Miraumont Road as the right flank, efforts were to be made to gain as much ground as possible, but not beyond Regina Trench. If necessary, the 8th Brigade and the remainder of the 9th Brigade would be used, as Regina Trench had to be gained at all costs. All available reserves were pushed up. The 60th, in support of the 9th Brigade, moved up two sections of bombers. The 43rd of this Brigade was ordered to assist the R.C.R. on their left in maintaining their position in Regina. The support Battalion of the

7th Brigade, the Princess Patricias, also moved up as close as possible.

Unfortunately, before a fresh offensive could be launched, reports began to come in that the R.C.R. had been unable to maintain their hold in Regina Trench. The men of the Princess Patricias sent up to reinforce the R.C.R. met the gallant defenders of the outpost returning to our trenches. A strong counter-attack had been too much for the weakened and wearied garrison. All returned together to Kenora Trench.

Early in the afternoon it became evident that the attack had failed all along the Corps' front. The line was consolidated during the night by the wearied troops in the line, aided by the supports. Little progress could be made on account of the weakness of the garrisons. On the left flank the depleted R.C.R. and 49th were combined into a composite Battalion.

On the following night the 8th Brigade relieved the 7th and 9th Brigades.

The undeniable failure of the operations of October 1st and 8th did not dishearten the Canadians. Rather did it merely increase their determination to "get" Regina, whatever the cost. It was intolerable that such a series of checks should follow the glorious triumph of Courcelette. Nevertheless, it is not to be wondered at that we should have met with these temporary checks, which were, indeed, far from diminishing the prestige of the Canadian Corps[3] as a fighting force. The victories of the 15th and immediately following days had had a double effect. They had severely reduced the numbers of the Canadian battalions while bringing them into contact with positions yet more formidably defended. At the same time they had forced the enemy to concentrate upon this sector, so imminently menaced, great reinforcements of men and guns. Their task had doubled, while their means of dealing with it had diminished. The quality of an army is sometimes manifested no less brilliantly in reverse than in success; and the scant result of these sanguinary struggles before Regina Trench in no way lessened the confidence of the Higher Command in the capacity of our troops.

A renewal of the offensive was daily expected, and active preparations were made in anticipation of the event. Meanwhile, the arrival of the new 4th Division during this period of waiting and recuperation was hailed by the hardened campaigners of the three older Divisions with feelings of liveliest satisfaction.

---

[3] The casualties of the Canadian Corps from noon, October 4th, to noon, October 11th, were as follows:—

OFFICERS.		OTHER RANKS.	
Killed	20	Killed	344
Wounded	109	Wounded	1,793
Missing	29	Missing	390
Total	158	Total	2,527

Total 2,685

CHAPTER IX

REGINA (CONTINUED)

The 4th Division, commanded by Major-General David Watson, C.B., C.M.G., entered the Somme area on October 10th and 11th, 1916, during the lull between the operations of October 8th and those of October 21st.

Though a new Division, which had never as yet taken part in any concerted major operations, it soon proved itself no whit inferior to the senior Divisions. It had had practical experience in holding the line in the Ypres salient in September, and it had already been blooded, for on the night of September 16th it had carried out a well-planned series of simultaneous raids which reflected the greatest credit on the new Division. There were seven raiding parties.

The first party consisted of one officer and forty men of the 22nd Battalion. Leaving the trenches at 11.22 p.m., the party moved cautiously forward, great care being necessary owing to the bright moonlight. The scaling ladders and chicken wire were left behind, as it was feared they might be seen too easily. As soon as the enemy trench was rushed the party split into two, working to the right and left. The enemy bolted so swiftly that only two were caught. Dug-outs were bombed and as much wire as possible destroyed by the covering party. At 12.25 a.m. the raiders left the enemy trench and found their way back without difficulty by means of the white tape laid for that purpose.

The 46th Battalion party of one officer and thirty-one other ranks carried out the second raid against the Hollandscheschuur Salient. At 12.20 a.m. the raiders crawled over the intervening space of forty yards, rushed the trench, and worked down to a supposed strong point. This proved to be merely a large hole, unstrengthened in any way. Explosives which had been brought to blow up this post were used against an occupied dug-out, 62 lb. of guncotton being touched off for the purpose. Fifteen Germans were killed during the raid and one captured. No difficulty was experienced in penetrating the wire.

The third raid was entrusted to the 47th Battalion. The raiding party of one officer and twenty-eight other ranks had further to go than the preceding parties and started five minutes earlier. Complete success was attained. The party bombed south after entering the enemy trench, making for a supposed strong point which turned out to be similar to the one above. Nine Germans were killed and ten taken prisoners.

The fourth raid was also undertaken by the 47th Battalion. A comparatively long distance separated the two trench lines, some 200 yards. On this account an early start was imperative. Scarcely any resistance was encountered. Six Germans were killed, and others were pursued but not caught. The artillery preparation, under Lieutenant-Colonel McNaughton, and the trench-mortar work were all that could be desired.

The 75th Battalion carried out the fifth raid. Three officers and thirty-one other ranks constituted the raiding party. They moved out just after midnight, formed up outside our wire, and were within twenty yards of the German trench while it was still being bombarded. Rushing in as soon as the barrage lifted, they divided up into two parties, which bombed right and left for fifty yards. Some resistance was encountered by the right party, but five of the enemy were killed, three captured, and the rest escaped over the parados under fire from the covering party. The left party also experienced resistance, but reached their objective in spite of opposition. Dug-outs were bombed and the enemy forced to escape over the parados. After a successful withdrawal the artillery was again turned on to the front line. Of the six prisoners taken four bolted on the way back and came to an untimely end. The 7th Belgian Field Artillery supporting the raid, rendered excellent service, which earned the warm commendation of all concerned in the operation.

The sixth raid, by the 54th Battalion was the most elaborate of all. Four officers and fifty-eight other ranks took part. The objective was No. 2 Crater at St. Eloi. Almost at the start the officers in charge were wounded. An unavoidable loss of direction and control naturally resulted, though the parties succeeded in reaching their objectives. An unfortunate *contretemps* arose from the fact that the bugler who was to have sounded the signal to retire fell into an exceedingly muddy and unsavoury shell-hole and lost his bugle! "A" party, on the left, captured three prisoners and bombed several inhabited dug-outs. A machine-gun was also captured. "B," "C," and "D" parties met with little resistance, and saw nothing of the enemy. "E" party bombed northwards towards No. 3 Crater, met with little opposition and captured one prisoner. "F" party had a harder task to the south on the far side of No. 3 Crater, but captured three prisoners and an automatic rifle, which was unfortunately lost when the man carrying it was wounded. "G" party, also moving south, unsuccessfully chased a number of the enemy towards the 75th raiding party.

As soon as the retirement began an undiscovered machine-gun opened up unexpectedly. Fifteen of the enemy were killed, including an officer and two men who resisted all attempts to bring them back after capture. Six prisoners were brought in.

The seventh raid, undertaken by the 87th Battalion, was unsuccessful. The three officers and forty-seven other ranks who made up the party got well away close under the barrage, but on reaching the parapet two small mines were exploded beneath them. In some way the enemy had become aware of the approaching raid, probably owing to an attack carried out by the Division on the left; the element of surprise, the great factor in all successful raids, was thus lost. Heavy fire was directed against the attackers; and after a brisk exchange of bombs it became evident that nothing could be accomplished. The party accordingly withdrew.

These raids, with the one exception noted, were eminently successful. This success was due in no small measure to the very careful preparation made beforehand. The parties involved were withdrawn from the line a week before the raid, all details were carefully worked out, trenches dug to scale, the ground constantly patrolled, and the raiding parties taken over it by night in small groups. The excellent artillery support and the thorough work of the covering parties all contributed to the satisfactory result.

On their arrival in the Somme area the 4th Division was fortunate enough to experience a few days of comparative quiet, with little more than shell-fire and sniping to incommode them while getting themselves shaken down into their new lines. Owing largely to the wretched weather, the conditions underfoot, and the state of the trenches, the operations pending, major and preliminary, were from day to day postponed. In fact, the three senior Canadian Divisions were withdrawn from the area before another attack in force was launched against the blood-drenched barrier of Regina. On October 17th the 4th Division, remaining behind, came under the orders of the II Corps for the purpose of future operations. These operations, in so far as the 4th Division was concerned, began on October 21st.

The general plan of operations was as follows. The II Corps[4] was to attack on the front between Courcelette Trench and the River Ancre in order to capture Petit Miraumont, Grandcourt, and at Pierre Divion. Afterwards the passages of the Ancre were to be forced and the II Corps would co-operate with the V Corps by pushing north. There were three Divisions in line, the 18th, 19th, and 39th, from right to left. The dual *rôle* of the 4th Canadian Division was to protect the right flank of the 18th Division of the II Corps and to safeguard the left flank of the III Corps on the right.

A preliminary operation was assigned to the II Corps before the general action began. This preparatory task was the capture of the Regina Stuff line of trenches, to be undertaken by the 18th, 25th, and 39th Divisions, from right to left. In this operation the 4th Canadian Division would co-operate by effecting the capture of Regina Trench from Courcelette Trench to a point just before the intersection of the Pys Road, thence approximately along an old German trench to join up with the sapheads which were being built by the 10th Canadian Infantry Brigade, under Brigadier-General William Hughes, D.S.O.

The 11th Brigade, on the left, under Brigadier-General V. W. Odlum, D.S.O., undertook the capture of the portion of Regina Trench assigned to the Division. Meanwhile, the 10th Brigade was to co-operate by pushing forward its saps so as to be able to support the 11th Brigade by an enfilading fire. Each Brigade, by the 19th, had completed a very useful sap, close to the junction of their respective lines, up old German trenches to within two-thirds of the distance to Regina. The 11th Brigade placed the 87th and 102nd Battalions in the line, the former on the right, each Battalion having two companies of the 75th in support.

At noon on the 21st the attack began. The whole operation was an unqualified success. Before the afternoon was far advanced the objectives had all been gained

[4] The II Corps consisted of the 18th, 19th, 25th, 39th British Divisions, and 4th Canadian Division.

and consolidated, blocks established in Regina and up the Pys Road, and contact effected with the equally successful 53rd Brigade of the 18th Division on the left. The co-operation of the 10th Brigade on the right was all that could be desired. Altogether the result of the action was a welcome change from the disappointments attending the hard-fought and determined attempts against Regina earlier in the month. The new and comparatively raw Division had won its spurs with *éclat*.

On the 25th of the month a second preliminary operation was undertaken. In preparation for this attack the right of the 10th Brigade was extended to the Chalk Pit.

At 7 a.m. the attacking Battalion, the 44th, advanced to the assault, supported by the 46th. Early reports seemed to indicate that the operation had been entirely successful. It soon became evident, however, that this was not the case. The enemy was enabled to hold his trenches in great force and to bring a devastatingly effective enfilading machine-gun fire to bear upon the 44th from the vicinity of the quadrangle. There was nothing for it but to take such cover as was available—old disused trenches and shell-holes, where many remained until dark. The Battalion suffered very heavily, having 3 officers killed and 7 wounded, and of other ranks 29 killed, 152 wounded, and 23 missing. The work of the stretcher-bearers in this action was especially commendable.

A long period of very bad weather compelled the postponement of further operation from day to day. Numerous operation orders and amending orders were issued, but nothing could be attempted until better weather conditions prevailed. It was decided that an attack on the remaining right section of Regina Trench would be made as soon as the weather should allow of two days' successful bombardment. On November 9th and 10th fine weather permitted good shooting. The plan of attack had been ready for some time in anticipation, and accordingly an assault was determined for the night of November 10th-11th.

From right to left the attacking line consisted of the 46th and 47th Battalions of the 10th Brigade and the 102nd Battalion of the 11th Brigade, attached for the purpose to the 10th Brigade. The aim was to capture and consolidate Regina Trench from the block established in Regina on the right flank of the 11th Brigade attack of October 21st to Farmer's Road. The 46th Battalion, on the right, attacked the line from the right boundary of the objective to the intersection of the Practice Road. The 47th Battalion was responsible for the central section. The 102nd Battalion, on the left, advanced against the remaining portion of Regina and also from the right extremity of the part of Regina already held in a north-easterly direction against the new enemy line running north and north-west from Regina to the Pys Road.

The 46th and 47th Battalions attacked at zero hour, midnight, with two companies each in line, in four waves. The company of the 102nd which advanced against Regina went forward in two waves, as did also the three platoons which attacked from Regina north-easterly towards the new German line.

The operation as a whole was very successful. The enemy's barrage was over the heads of the attacking troops, who stole a march on their opponents, for zero hour found them 150 yards in advance of their front trench, so that they were in amongst the Germans almost before the Huns realised what was happening. In the centre success was immediate and complete, though the 47th suffered more severely than the other Battalions for the reason that they were the only Battalion to run into heavy machine-gun fire. On the right the 46th was equally victorious, but they encountered a stiffer resistance. Good fortune also favoured the attack of the 102nd Battalion on the left. The specified portion of Regina was captured, and the northern attacking party was also, at first, completely successful; later, however, they were bombed back some distance, and established a block about 85 yards in advance of Regina. This post was stoutly held against a number of determined counter-attacks.

By 1.20 a.m. the 46th and 47th had overrun their objective, and dug in some 100 yards beyond it. Unfortunately, this new line came under our own protective artillery fire, and had to be abandoned. By 2.20 a.m., however, consolidation was well advanced. The required posts were established, and work started on new connecting saps and trenches. The working party which the O.C. 46th had been ordered to detail came up on time, and everything was rapidly rounding into shape, including the new connecting trench between Regina and Kling Trenches.

At daybreak a concentration by the enemy in Below and New Gallwitz Trenches was dispersed by our artillery. Conditions rapidly became normal, and it was now possible to take stock of the position. Altogether it had been a notable success for the 4th Division.

The casualties in the 10th Brigade were 3 officers killed and 4 wounded, and 41 other ranks killed, 156 wounded, and 26 missing. The majority of these were of the 47th Battalion.

The 102nd Battalion of the 11th Brigade had 4 officers wounded, 10 other ranks killed, 34 wounded, and 8 missing.

Three officers and 84 other ranks were captured, also 4 machine-guns. About 50 German dead were found in the trench; and, in addition, they lost a number of men who endeavoured to escape across country.

Regina Trench itself proved a disappointment. It was knee-deep in mud, and some of the dug-outs had only been commenced. In addition to the capture of Regina, the advanced salient shown on the map was pushed out in order to secure observation of Coulée and Below Trenches.

All concerned in the operation received the congratulations of the Higher Command. The whole of Regina Trench, which had defied the Canadian Corps for over a month, was now in British hands; and the 4th Canadian Division had earned an enviable reputation for a young Division—-a reputation which was to be further enhanced by the achievement of the 11th Brigade a week later.

On November 18th this Brigade, taking part in the resumed general offensive, carried out its task of capturing and consolidating Desire Trench. The whole operation, which is described in the succeeding chapter, was executed with dash and thoroughness, and brought to a fitting conclusion the strenuous campaign of the Canadian Divisions on the Somme.

CHAPTER X

DESIRE TRENCH

Throughout the closing operations against Regina Trench our Battalions had been forced to pluck every hard success from the teeth of a new foe who had come suddenly to the support of the German defence. This foe was the mud, the hated Somme mud, deep, slithering, tenacious as glue, foul with all the filth left behind by the enemy as he gave back yard by yard. For the weather had turned against us. The rains of the rainiest autumn which had scourged their high plateaus for many a year were a timely reinforcement to the hard-pressed enemy. When it came to the attack upon Desire Trench, on November 17th-18th, the disastrous alliance of mud and rain-drench had reached such a pitch of obstruction that the capture of this line was reluctantly recognised as marking the limit of our possible advance, for the time, upon this sector. The light railways, spread over the vast, red, undulating expanses of naked mud, between the engulfing and omnipresent pits of slime, were being constantly scattered and put out of service by the German shells from north and east—from beyond the Ancre and from the hidden batteries in Lupart Wood; and they were utterly incapable of keeping up the ammunition supply for our valiant advanced batteries of 18-pounders. Our heavies, the great 9.2 howitzers lurking in and around the tossed ruins of Pozières and behind Courcelette, were well supplied, thanks to the indefatigable labours of the road-making companies along the great and crowded artery of the Bapaume Road. But the 18-pounders, in their shallow gun-pits far out across the shell-swept stretches of the mud, had to be fed by pack-mules, carrying shells in panniers slung across the back. Such a method of transport was torturingly slow, and perilous to the last degree, but it was the only one capable of coping with the situation. Under the numbing strain the spirit and humour of our men remained irrepressible, as instanced in the following retort to a sentry's challenge. Under the chill downpour of the unrelenting rain, through the blind night, a soldier, just returned from four days' duty in the front trenches, came stumbling in along the Bapaume Road toward the billets of Albert. Shrapnel helmet, overcoat, pack, everything but his precious rifle, was covered thick with that chalky mud which sticketh closer than a brother, and he waded heavily through the mire of the tormented roadway. He reached a dripping sentry. "Halt! Who goes there?" came the challenge, as the labouring figure lurched up in the gloom. "Submarine U13," grunted the traveller. "Pass, Submarine U13," responded the sentry cheerfully; and the moving shape of mud rolled on toward the shattered billets brooded over by the falling Virgin and Child.

Under such conditions, but in such unshakable temper, the men of the 4th

Canadian Division moved to the taking of the position known as Desire Support Trench, on which for days they had been casting covetous eyes. Our objective lay across our whole Divisional front, from about Farmer's Road on the right to some 600 yards west of the West Miraumont Road on the left. At this point our left flank made connection with the 18th Division, which was to attack, simultaneously with our advance, the western sector of Desire Trench, and other trenches which were protecting the approaches to Grandcourt Village. The right of our attack—a frontage of only five or six hundred yards, but one offering extreme difficulties—was confided to the 10th Brigade, under Brigadier-General W. St. P. Hughes. The left, and main, sector, beginning at the Pys Road, was committed to the 11th Brigade, under Brigadier-General V. W. Odlum, who had two Battalions from the 12th Brigade, the 38th and the 78th, attached to his command. There were thus three Battalions engaged upon the right sector, and five upon the left. The 10th Brigade, with its restricted frontage and limited objective, attacked with two companies of the 50th Battalion (Calgary Regiment, Lieutenant-Colonel E. G. Mason) and one company and one platoon of the 46th (South Saskatchewan Regiment, Lieutenant-Colonel H. J. Dawson) in the assaulting waves, with one company of the 44th (Winnipeg, Lieutenant-Colonel E. K. Wayland) in support. General Odlum made his attack with four Battalions, each represented by two companies in the assaulting wave, and one Battalion, behind his centre, in support. The attacking Battalions, from right to left, were as follows:—The 75th (Mississaugas Battalion, of Toronto, Lieutenant-Colonel S. G. Beckett), 54th (Kootenay Regiment, Lieutenant-Colonel A. G. H. Kemball), 87th (Canadian Grenadier Guards, Montreal, Lieutenant-Colonel R. W. Frost), and 38th of the 12th Brigade (Ottawa, Lieutenant-Colonel C. M. Edwards); while the Battalion supporting was the 78th (Manitoba, Lieutenant-Colonel J. Kirkcaldie), also of the 12th Brigade. The artillery supporting the operation consisted of the 1st, 2nd, and 3rd Canadian Divisional Artillery (commanded respectively by Brigadier-General H. C. Thacker, C.M.G., Brigadier-General E. W. B. Morrison, and Lieutenant-Colonel J. H. Mitchell), the Yukon Motor Machine-Gun Battery (Captain H. F. Murling), and also by the 11th Divisional Artillery and the 2nd Corps Heavy Artillery.

The barrage work of the artillery was admirably co-ordinated, and effectually cleared the way for that success which so abundantly rewarded the operation as a whole in spite of failure on the extreme right. While a concentrated standing barrage was flaming and crashing along the whole line of the enemy trench, at the hour for launching the attack (6.10 a.m.) a creeping barrage was put up along a line 200 yards in front of our own parapets. This line of roaring death rolled onward at the rate of 50 yards per minute, with the first wave of our assault following close behind it—so close, in their eagerness, that a sergeant swore he might have lighted his pipe at it. Presently this barrage merged into the standing barrage along the German trench. At fourteen minutes after the launching of the attack the combined barrage lifted from the doomed trench and rolled inexorably onward for another 250 yards, where it rested as a barrier against counter-attacks. The trench was seized, all opposition being swiftly overwhelmed, and our men rushed on behind the barrage to a distance of 150 yards beyond the captured line. Here they hurriedly dug themselves in, knowing that the Germans would begin to shell Desire itself as soon as it should be reported that we had captured it. In order that the enemy might not discover our ruse in time to thwart it, a dense smoke-screen was flung out by a special company of the Royal Engineers in front of the line where our men were furiously digging. The positions thus gained, about 150 yards beyond Desire, were consolidated and held; and they stood to mark the limit of Canada's advance on the Somme.

So much, in brief, for the battle of Desire Trench. Viewed as a whole, it was a rounded and clean-cut success, and earned warm commendation for General Watson and his hard-fighting 4th Division. To get an idea of the fluctuations of the struggle, it is necessary to take the operations of the 10th and 11th Brigades separately.

The task assigned to the 10th Brigade, as already stated, was an attack on a very narrow but extremely exposed and strongly defended objective. The whole line of this objective lay open to concentrated artillery fire from the enemy's rear, and was murderously cross-raked by the fire from a number of machine-gun nests. It proved, in the event, difficult to carry and impossible to hold. But this comparative failure, happily, did not vitiate the success of the main operation, which lay along the left front.

The 50th Battalion, occupying the Brigade left, made its advance successfully to a depth of some 300 yards, and gained its objective with small loss. This objective was a line running east from the Pys Road. Here, however, it got involved in our own smoke barrage, lost its direction (and consequently its touch with the troops on its left), swerved to the right, and left an open gap of about 200 yards between the two Brigades. Then the German guns from Lupart Wood in front opened an annihilating fire upon it, machine-guns swept it from both sides, and it was forced back with a loss of 12 officers and 200 other ranks—over half its total strength in the attack.

Meanwhile, the 46th Battalion, on the right, was faring no better. The attack was made by one company and one platoon, in two waves, on a front of 100 yards. There was a distance of 40 yards between the waves. The first wave, keeping a fair line in spite of the shell-holes, escaped the German barrage, and got to within 70 yards of the enemy's parapets with small loss. Here, however, it was met by massed rifle fire full in the face—for our own barrage at this point was playing behind instead of upon the German trench, and the trench was occupied in full force. At the same time a torrent of machine-gun fire opened up on the left. The wave was broken. The survivors took refuge in shell-holes, where they had to lie all day under a ceaseless storm of shell and bullets, till darkness enabled them to crawl back to our lines. The second wave fared even worse. It was caught by the enemy's barrage as it was coming over the parapet. Torn and diminished, it nevertheless rushed on, in the face of intolerable punishment, till it was a line no longer. Its remnants made their way into a sap and crept back into Regina. Later in the day, however, the Brigade was able to thrust forward again for a short distance on the left, toward the Pys Road, and so to contain the position which it had failed to capture. Thus contained the position ceased to be of service to the enemy or any serious menace to our new line on the left; and day or two afterwards it was simply pounded out of existence by a "combined shoot" of all our heavy guns.

In the main attack, all along the line westward from Pys Road, things went well from the start. By 7.30 reports came back from the 75th, 54th, and 38th Battalions that all were in their objectives and busy consolidating their gains. The only mystery was in regard to the 87th, which though apparently successful, had disappeared. While this matter was in doubt the Germans launched a counter-attack from Coulée Trench against the 54th Battalion. They advanced with a great show of resolution several hundred yards, then suddenly, to our astonishment, flung down their bombs and rifles, threw up their hands, and rushed into our line as eager prisoners. About 8.50 came news that the 38th Battalion, not content with having captured its objective, had pushed on and gained a section of Grandcourt Trench, where it was establishing itself successfully. Then about 9 o'clock the mystery of the 87th was solved. This Battalion also, feeling that it had not had enough had gone on to try conclusions with Grandcourt Trench, and made good its footing there.

These fine adventures of the 38th and 87th, however, were doomed to prove fruitless of result. The operation of the Canadians against Desire Trench was, as we have seen, part of a wider movement, extending far to the left, before Grandcourt Village. The 18th Division, on our immediate left, though worn with long fighting and far below strength, had made good upon its right, where it joined our lines, but had been held up by insurmountable obstacles near Grandcourt. For this reason the Higher Command decided that it would be inadvisable to attempt to hold such an advanced position as the 38th and 87th had taken in Grandcourt Trench. In the course of the day, therefore, came orders that all advanced units were to come back to their original first objectives and consolidate there. The line of Desire Trench, thus gained and secured, was an admirable one, strong for defence, and advantageous to attack from when next the occasion should offer itself. And on this line the 4th Division rested until, at the end of the month, they were relieved and moved back to Doullens. The casualties of the Division in this fine action amounted to 75 officers and 1,276 other ranks. The prisoners taken numbered 625, of whom 17 were officers. The Division received warm congratulations from the Commanders of the Corps and the Army upon the success of this its concluding operation in the blood-drenched battlefields of the Somme.

From these fields the Canadian Forces, the four Divisions henceforth united into an Army Corps in all respects complete within itself, were removed to the north of Arras, to take into their competent keeping that vital area lying under the menace of Vimy Ridge and the impregnable outposts of Lens.

Welded now by sacrifice, endurance, prudent and brilliant leaderships, and glorious achievements against the mightiest military Power in the world's history, into a fighting force of incomparable effectiveness, it was no less than their due that the most tremendous tasks should be set to these fiery and indomitable fighters of the North. To the Canadian Battalions the impregnable and the invincible had come to mean a challenge which they welcomed joyously. They knew that the utmost of which men were capable was now confidently expected of them. How gloriously they were to justify that high expectation, on the dreadful Ridge of Vimy, amid the bloody slag-heaps of Lens, and along the fire-swept crest of Passchendaele, remains to be told succeeding volumes of their story.

APPENDIX

CHRONOLOGICAL INDEX.

SEPTEMBER 1ST - NOVEMBER 28TH, 1917.

The Canadian Corps on the Somme.

September 1st.

1st Canadian Division arrives at the Somme, with headquarters at Rubempré. 1st Canadian Infantry Brigade takes over right section of line south-west of Courcelette, under orders of the 4th Australian Division.

September 2nd.

2nd Infantry Brigade moves to Brickfields under orders of the 4th Australian Division.

September 3rd.

3rd Infantry Brigade is instructed to establish a line on the left section from a point on the Mouquet Road to north of Mouquet Farm to the north-west and round the farm to the south. Command of the Canadian Corps area in the Ypres salient passes to the G.O.C. 1st Anzac Corps, and command of the line north-east of Albert is assumed by the G.O.C. Canadian Corps.

Canadians very busy patrolling, reconnoitring, and locating enemy lines.

September 4th.

1st Canadian Division relieves 4th Australian Division at Tara Hill. The stubborn fighting round Mouquet Farm commences and our men repulse an attack west of Mouquet. Patrols from the 13th Battalion enter enemy's line and block communication trenches.

September 5th.

1st Divisional Artillery relieves the 2nd Australian Divisional Artillery. 3rd and 1st Brigades in front line with reserves in Quarry and Tom's Cut, Centre Way and Union Trench. A very heavy hostile artillery fire hampers our communications, and scores a direct hit on 3rd Brigade Headquarters. The G.O.C. orders Mouquet Farm to be taken.

September 6th.

The enemy shell the left sector heavily, later extending an intense bombardment over the whole front line and area. A large party of Germans advancing from the direction of Courcelette is dispersed by our artillery.

September 7th.

Preparations for operation on the 9th. Our patrols very busy. Enemy shell Mouquet Farm sectors heavily, obliterating Kay Trench, and our artillery retaliates on Zollern Redoubt. The Royal Flying Corps reports enemy communications full of troops and our guns open heavily upon the Courcelette communication trenches. 2nd Division arrives at the Somme.

September 8th.

2nd Brigade relieves 3rd Brigade. Early in the morning while relief is in progress the enemy attack Mouquet Road and drive our men back. Later in the day a strong attack is defeated by our bombers and machine-gun fire. The fighting round Mouquet continues in the evening—the Germans repulsed.

Extract from Reserve Army S.G. 21/0/35 Sept. 8/16.—Object of Canadian Corps operations is to advance our line in co-operation with III Corps until we can obtain direct observation from as many points as possible over German third line running Flers—Le Sars—Pys.

September 9th.

At 4.45 p.m. the 2nd Battalion attacks successfully south-west of Courcelette from vicinity of Windmill to Munster Alley, gaining objectives and capturing two machine-guns and some eighty prisoners. The enemy's counter-attacks repulsed and the captured area consolidated.

September 10th.

Enemy massing troops and bombarding our line heavily. Our artillery barrage along the Pozières-Bapaume Road effectively breaks up hostile formation against 1st Brigade. On the left sector the 2nd Brigade drives back several German raids, repulsing a strong and determined attack from Mouquet Farm. 3rd Canadian Division arrived at the Somme.

September 11th.

2nd Division relieves 1st Division in right sector. Early in the morning the 4th Brigade defeats an attempt to rush our posts established in front of the line captured on the 9th. Pozières bombarded with gas shells.

September 12th.

Canadian Corps takes over new area—the Ovillers-Courcelette Road and the ground south of it to Moy Avenue.

An intense hostile bombardment causes many casualties amongst our working parties. On the Mouquet sectors the 2nd Brigade is relieved by the 8th Brigade, 3rd Division, including the 2nd Canadian Mounted Rifles, who repulse another strong attack from Mouquet Farm in the evening.

September 13th.

Our artillery preparing the way for the attack. The Germans appear to be very nervous and many deserters come into our lines at night. The 4th, 6th, and 8th Brigade, 2nd and 3rd Division, holding the front line.

Orders issued for attack on the 15th. The Canadian Corps Cavalry anticipating work. The enemy advance in numbers against the sector held by the 1st and 5th Canadian Mounted Rifles, but the heavy artillery effectively breaks up the attack.

September 14th.

Artillery active, but little infantry work. The 2nd Division to attack Courcelette and the 3rd Division Fabeck Graben. It was hoped that the cavalry might penetrate the German lines east of Courcelette and disable communications and guns round Pys and Grandcourt, but after much reconnaissance and patrol work the country was found impracticable for mounted men.

September 15th.

General offensive at 6.20 a.m. by six battalions of the 2nd and 3rd Divisions. The whole objective secured by 10 a.m., and the attack continues successfully in the afternoon, resulting in a line being established from the point of the original salient east of Mouquet via Fabeck Trench to west end of Courcelette then around north and east side of village down to Gunpit Trench to the north-west corner of Martinpuich. The tanks, in action for the first time, help to secure a brilliant success.

The Commander-in-Chief congratulates the Canadians.

September 16th.

Consolidation of occupied areas. The 4th Brigade in position along Gunpit Trench with the 5th Brigade on its left, and the 8th Brigade along the Mouquet Farm sectors. Orders issued to the 2nd Division to push forward and establish posts in advance trenches north-north-east of Courcelette. The 3rd Division to be prepared to capture the line of the Zollern Graben to Festen Zollern—and Mouquet Farm. The Germans massing troops and hostile barrages damage our communications. In the evening the 2nd Canadian Mounted Rifles surround Mouquet Farm. At 5 p.m. the Royal Canadian Rifles and the 42nd Battalion attack the Zollern Graben Trench but are driven back.

The 46th British Infantry Brigade takes over the Gunpit Trench line to the Bapaume Road, relieving the 4th Brigade.

September 17th.

Our men repulse several counter-attacks. Early in the morning the 34th British Infantry Brigade relieves the 8th Brigade, taking over the Mouquet Farm sector. In the afternoon the 5th Brigade attacks east of Courcelette, at the same time sending a bombing raid up Sunken Road. Small successful offensives help to clear up our positions, though the hostile artillery fire tries our men severely. The 5th Brigade holding frontage from Bapaume Road to Courcelette Cemetery, to Main Street to Sunken Road to Cross Roads north-west of village.

Extract from Reserve Army S.G.21/0/45.—"Canadian Corps will establish posts on all the high ground north and north-west of Courcelette and gain observation over the Ancre Valley and especially over the enemy trenches in R23 and 22, trenches round Courcelette Road, north of Hessian Trench, Grandcourt Road and vicinity."

September 18th.

2nd Division is relieved by 1st Division. Our men establishing bombing and machine-gun posts north of Courcelette under a heavy artillery fire. Hostile bombing parties driven back.

September 19th.

At 9.30 p.m. the enemy attack north-east of Courcelette and gain a footing in our trenches. A counter-attack organised by the 4th Battalion and the line recaptured, though a few advanced posts remain in possession of the enemy.

September 20th.

At 4 a.m. a further attack along this whole frontage is made by the enemy, but is repulsed by machine-gun fire and bombs. Later, the 58th and 43rd Battalions, 3rd Division attack the Zollern Graben Line and after severe fighting succeed in entering the trench. Fighting stubbornly, our men repulse four counter-attacks, until at last, after an intense bombardment, the Germans come on in great numbers under cover of a smoke barrage and force the Canadians back to their starting point.

September 21st.

Our barrages check a very heavy enemy fire on Sunken Road and the right front line, though a German battery succeeds in blowing up the ammunition dump at La Boiselle.

1st and 9th Brigades holding front line.

September 22nd.

In the evening an attack made by the 4th Battalion, 1st Brigade against the maze of German trenches immediately east of Courcelette. This objective secured and some prisoners taken. Patrols from the 9th Brigade establish posts in High Trench West. The Canadians holding a line from a point near Mouquet Road in the Fabeck Graben Trench to north-west Courcelette, to north Courcelette, round the Quarry and east of the village towards Martinpuich.

September 23rd.

1st and 2nd Brigades in front line. The Canadian Corps anxious to push forward towards Le Sars line and 1st Division is instructed to work up the trench north of Bapaume Road to join with the British 23rd Division attacking north of

Martinpuich. (M.26).

September 24th.

1st Brigade holding Bapaume Road to north-east Courcelette. 2nd and 3rd Brigades round Quarry, north of Courcelette to Fabeck Graben. (R.28.c.3.6.) Continued severe bombardment of our lines. A strong enemy patrol attacks our new post on the Bapaume Road, but is repulsed, though another attack gains him footing in our advanced posts near the Cemetery.

September 25th.

1st and 2nd Divisions in front line preparing for offensive. Canadian Corps to co-operate with II. Corps in capture of ridge running north-west of Courcelette to the Schwaben Redoubt. The 2nd Division objective a new German trench north of Courcelette—the 1st Division to take the Kenora and Regina Trenches by way of the Zollern and Hessian lines. Later the 1st Division objective is shortened and changed to a point on the West Miraumont Road.

September 26th.

At 12.35 p.m. the 1st and 2nd Divisions attack and, after heavy fighting, partially occupy the Zollern, Hessian, and Kenora Trenches. On the right the 29th and 31st Battalions are held up in their operations north of Courcelette, but after several determined attacks succeed in gaining their objective. The enemy resist stubbornly, and during the night bombard Courcelette and the whole front line. The left of the 2nd Brigade is badly hampered in its operations by machine-gun fire from Mouquet Farm and Stuff Redoubt. Representations made to the 11th British Division on the left, who, at 6.30 p.m., report the official clearing up to the Farm.

September 27th.

In the morning the 2nd Brigade attacked the Hessian Trench and drove the Germans back towards Regina Trench, only to lose the greater part of their gain in a strong hostile counter-attack about 1 p.m. A fresh attack was made in the afternoon and the whole regained and held. At 6.30 p.m. it was reported that the Germans had withdrawn from their line between the Bapaume Road and the Courcelette Trench, and our patrols were busy establishing posts in the North and South Practice Trenches, along the Dyke Road, and towards Regina Trench between the east and west Miraumont Roads.

On the left hostile reinforcements had arrived and driven the 14th Battalion from Kenora Trench to a line of defence some 200 yards south-west.

September 28th.

Cavalry reconnaissances find enemy in Destremont Farm and in strength in the Le Sars line. 4th Brigade pushing forward north of Courcelette, and bombing parties fighting their way towards Regina. On the left the 1st Division repulses a determined attack against our Hessian Trench and our posts about Kenora Trench. Our line in process of construction from Bapaume Road to Dyke Road to East

Miraumont Road to a point 150 yards up Courcelette Trench and south to Kenora Trench, to Hessian as far as the Courcelette Road. The enemy massing troops, and an intense bombardment by our artillery silences many batteries and breaks up hostile formations. 4th, 5th, 6th, and 8th Brigades in front line.

September 29th.

At 5.15 a.m. a further strong attack upon Hessian Trench repulsed by our men, and about noon the 2nd Canadian Mounted Rifles, in co-operation with the British Brigade on the Canadian left, attack and capture the German communication from Hessian Trench to Courcelette Road. A strong post established. Very heavy hostile artillery fire and incessant fighting for small gains. 2nd Division instructed to occupy and consolidate a line from Destremont Farm and North and South Practice Trenches.

September 30th.

4th, 5th, and 8th Brigades in front line. Enemy working hard building defences. 8th Brigade takes over 5th Brigade lines to Twenty-three Road, and preparations are made for new offensive.

Extract from Reserve Army S.G. 66/8. 30/9/16.—"The operations of the Reserve Army will comprise two simultaneous attacks.

"(*a*) A southern attack by the Canadian Corps to capture Irles. The right of this attack will rest on the Bois Loupart (inclusive). The left of the attack will, in the early stages, be held back on the high ground overlooking Miraumont.

"(*b*) A western attack by the V. and XIII. Corps...."

October 1st.

4th, 5th, and 8th Brigades, 2nd and 3rd Divisions in front line. At 3.20 p.m. the Canadians attack a line from Destremont Farm to the junction of the Courcelette and Regina Trenches, thence the line of the Regina Trench through Twenty-three Road to the Courcelette Road and south to the Hessian Trench.

Our troops penetrate into this objective in certain localities, but unable to maintain themselves. The 5th Canadian Mounted Rifles on the left succeed in bombing down Regina Trench nearly as far as the West Miraumont Road, but a heavily-reinforced counter-attack drives them back to Hessian Trench about 6 p.m. However, our troops succeed in establishing a new line from the Courcelette Trench across the Pys Road, thence running north and north-east of the Practice Trenches and across the Dyke Road to a junction with the British Division on the Canadian right. Kenora Trench held to a few yards from Regina and posts established forward in Courcelette Trench.

October 2nd.

Royal Flying Corps reports that the enemy is very strong along Regina Trench on the west of the East Miraumont Road. Special reconnaissance ordered of Regina Trench from the East Miraumont Road to the Le Sars line. Our troops very busy establishing the new line and Regina Trench is shelled heavily by our artillery. A new line ordered to be established from which to attack Regina Trench between Courcelette Trench and Below Trench.

October 3rd.

5th Brigade relieved by the 6th. Our advanced post in Kenora close to Regina Trench is abandoned temporarily in order to allow the artillery a free hand. A night reconnaissance of Regina Trench produced little result owing to the intense darkness. Reserve Army decides to postpone operations planned for Oct. 5th as more time is required for artillery preparation. Work is actively continued on the new line in front of Regina Trench in spite of the heavy rain.

October 4th.

Zollern Trench and the front areas heavily shelled by the hostile artillery. The Royal Canadian Rifles occupy Kendall Trench and establish posts within a few yards of the enemy. 3rd Division assumes command of 2nd Division lines.

October 5th.

4th Canadian Division arrives at the Somme. Canadian artillery bombards Regina Trench heavily. Our men busy digging new jumping-off trenches in preparation for a new offensive, and patrols and aeroplanes reconnoitring.

October 6th.

9th Brigade relieved by 7th Brigade. 3rd Division sends out patrols along Regina Trench examining wire.

Reconnaissance made of Destremont line, 1st Division assumes command of the Destremont Farm front. The enemy bombarding Courcelette and Maple Leaf Road.

October 7th.

3rd Canadian Divisional Artillery arrives at the Somme and relieves the Lahore Artillery.

1st and 3rd Divisions in front line. Artillery active on both sides—and our troops completing preparations for the attack. Patrols work along Twenty-three Road from the junction on Regina and Kenora Trenches and report enemy's wire in fairly good condition.

October 8th.

At 4.50 a.m. the 1st and 3rd Divisions attack the German positions from Dyke Road around the Quadrilateral (the intersection of Gallwitz Trench and support, and Below Trench and support), thence along Regina Trench to the Kenora communication between the Grandcourt and Twenty-three Roads. The two right battalions reach their objectives and on the left the 7th and 9th Brigades gained a footing in the German lines. However, it is found impossible to hold the positions against the vigorous counter-attacks of the enemy, and after stubborn fighting the

Canadians are forced back to their jumping-off trenches.

October 9th.

The 1st Division constructs a new trench south of the Quadrilateral from Dyke Road to Below Trench, at which point junction is made with the British Brigade on the right. The enemy shell the whole front area with shrapnel and high explosive.

October 10th.

8th Brigade patrols busy along the line of Regina Trench. Hostile bombardment of Dyke Road and North Practice Trenches, but our troops actively continue the construction and consolidation of the new lines. Patrols report the strong condition of the enemy wire. 2nd Division leaves the Somme.

October 11th.

Very heavy hostile bombardment of the 8th Brigade front and support trenches from Twenty-three Road to north of the North Practice Trenches, causing severe damage to the trenches and somewhat heavy casualties. Near the East Miraumont Road the Germans attempt an attack from Regina Trench, but the barrage of the 2nd Divisional Artillery prevents them from leaving their own parapet. Parties of Germans driven by our artillery fire from Regina Trench are caught on the Pys and East Miraumont Road by our 18-pounders and engaged with excellent effect. Later on our artillery disperses another large party near the Grandcourt Road.

The G.O.C. 4th Division assumes command of 3rd Division lines, with the 8th Brigade remaining under orders of the 4th Division.

October 12th.

Our new trench south of the Quadrilateral between Dyke Road and Below Trench suffers a heavy bombardment. Our artillery active in wire cutting and a deliberate shelling of the enemy defences. Gas and lachrymatory shells thrown into Courcelette and Pozières.

October 13th.

Little infantry activity, though patrols are busy preparing for the proposed offensive. The enemy bombard Martinpuich, and our front and support areas, with heavy retaliation by our artillery.

October 14th.

4th Divisional sector shelled heavily, with the enemy throwing gas shells into the 8th Brigade lines. Left Brigade trenches damaged and communications cut by an intense barrage during the afternoon. Canadian Corps decides to postpone the planned attack.

October 15th.

53rd British Infantry Brigade relieves 8th Brigade on the left of the line. Our heavy artillery directs an intense fire upon Regina, Courcelette, Below, and Gallwitz Trenches, doing a great deal of damage to the hostile defences and causing many casualties. The village of Pys bombarded also, and many enemy observation posts demolished. A large party of Germans observed near Achiet Trench and broken up by our artillery fire. Patrols from the 10th and 11th Brigades examine wire in front of Regina Trench in spite of the heavy bombardment.

October 16th.

Very satisfactory damage to the enemy's barbed wire reported by the 4th Division patrols. A quiet day for the infantry, but our artillery silences several hostile batteries and causes many casualties in a body of infantry observed north of Irles. Regina, Coulée, and Courcelette Trenches bombarded and machine-gun emplacements successfully located and destroyed.

October 17th.

10th Brigade, 4th Division, takes over 2nd Brigade, 1st Division, lines. 4th Canadian Division comes under command of II. Corps and receives instructions for the preliminary operations. The 11th Brigade to capture and consolidate Regina Trench from Courcelette Trench to a point just before the junction with the Pys Road, then easterly to the sapheads built by the 10th Brigade. Strong blocks to be pushed out along the East Miraumont Road and the German trenches running parallel to it. The 10th Brigade to push forward its saps towards Regina and co-operate with the 11th Brigade with machine-gun fire. The artillery active on both sides, the enemy shelling the 10th Brigade front rather heavily.

October 18th.

The arrangements for the offensive on the 19th practically completed. The 11th Brigade moves up to its advanced headquarters in the North Practice Trenches, and has a great deal of trouble establishing satisfactory communications. Artillery not very busy, though our guns keep the enemy from repairing his damaged defences.

October 19th.

A steady rain, making movement almost impossible over the heavy ground. The 2nd Army decides to postpone the attack for twenty-four hours. The 10th and 11th Brigades working hard driving saps towards Regina Trench and establishing jumping-off positions. The 11th Brigade lines shelled heavily and continuously, despite the retaliation of the Canadian artillery.

October 20th.

Operations postponed for a further twenty-four hours, and the artillery takes advantage of the delay to complete the demolition of the enemy's wire. A quiet day for the infantry, but the trenches are full of water and in very bad condition, necessitating ceaseless work. The 3rd Canadian Division leaves the Somme area.

October 21st.

Attack made about noon by the 11th Brigade, excellent machine-gun work materially aiding a most successful offensive. The whole objective gained, and by 2 p.m. our men are busy consolidating the captured area. Enemy massing near the Coulée Trench dispersed by our artillery fire. Further information received that the Germans are concentrating near the Chalk pits east of the Quadrilateral, and artillery and machine-gun barrages redoubled and a counter-attack prevented.

The 1st Canadian Division leaves the Somme area.

October 22nd.

No attempt made by the enemy to counter-attack during the night, beyond a few bombing raids which were easily repulsed. The 10th Brigade to complete the capture of Regina Trench. The state of the front lines is very bad and our men work under the most trying conditions. The enemy shell the captured areas heavily.

October 23rd.

Preparations for the Big Push in process of completion. The 10th Brigade is instructed to extend its right to the Chalk Pit south of Warlencourt, and the preliminary attack arranged for the 24th. 11th Brigade to co-operate by pushing up the block in Regina Trench eastwards. Dyke Road heavily shelled.

October 24th.

The 10th Brigade reports that the 44th Battalion, instructed to capture the remainder of Regina, is very much exhausted by the severe conditions, and the minor operation is postponed for twenty-four hours. 11th Brigade patrols push their block in Regina another 120 yards eastwards.

October 25th.

At 7 a.m. the 44th Battalion attack the portion of Regina Trench remaining in German hands—between the Quadrilateral and the 11th Brigade block east of the Pys Road—but meeting with very heavy enfilading machine-gun fire from the Quadrilateral the men are quite unable to reach their objective. The 11th Brigade have bombed eastwards from the block in Regina but as the 44th Battalion do not arrive the Germans are enabled to concentrate a strong bombing counter-attack and drive our men back to their original post. The Corps decides to make this portion of the Regina Trench part of the objective in the later operation.

October 26th.

The 12th Brigade relieves the 10th and 11th Brigades in the line. Hostile artillery active south of the Albert- Bapaume Road. German troops observed in large numbers in the Grandcourt Trench and our heavy guns concentrate on this point.

October 27th.

Operations postponed once more. The Germans endeavouring to complete new defensive works between the Regina and Grandcourt Trenches, but making little headway, owing to our continued artillery and machine-gun fire.

October 28th.

Enemy shelling vigorously in the area south of the Albert-Bapaume Road. The 78th Battalion sends out patrols to locate new enemy lines. The roads are very bad, and great difficulty is experienced in transporting the ammunition to the guns.

October 29th.

The bad weather prevents operations, but our artillery and machine-gun barrages effectually prevent the Germans from working on their new defences.

October 30th.

Gale blowing and artillery work hampered. Operations postponed until November 5th. Heavy rain renders the condition of the front trenches indescribable, and frequent reliefs have to be made.

October 31st.

Weather improves, and the artillery fire becomes general. The enemy shell Albert, while our guns are busy wire-cutting and destroying German defences. Satisfactory reports received on the state of the wire in front of Coulée and Below Trenches.

November 1st.

Bad weather continues to hamper our artillery work, though the enemy shell our support lines and communication trenches. The 10th Brigade sends out patrols to intercept and cut up hostile working parties. The roads are very bad, and operations are postponed until Nov. 7th.

November 2nd.

Patrol penetrates north between Pys and Miraumont Road for some 500 yards. Weather clears and aircraft and artillery correspondingly busy. Enemy working parties dispersed and their defensive work prevented.

November 3rd.

12th Brigade relieved by 10th and 11th Brigades. Fair observation, and artillery active on both sides. Observation patrol reaches a point north of the Destremont Road and reports that the German wire in front of Gallwitz Trench is not a formidable obstacle.

November 4th.

Hostile aerial activity, and much movement of troops and transport observed in the German lines along the Irles-Miraumont Road. 10th and 11th Brigade patrols work up East Miraumont Road and to the east, some of our men reaching Gallwitz Trench. German wire appears to be badly damaged by our artillery fire. Enemy hard at work improving his defences.

November 5th.

British and Australians attacking the Butte de Warlencourt on the Canadian right and the enemy place a barrage on the 10th Brigade lines. Patrol report that the Germans have thrown out new wire in front of their new trench north of the Quadrilateral, running east from Below Trench—but that there appear to be no obstacles to our advance on a line from Practice Road to a point 200 yards east of Farmer Road.

November 6th.

The 10th Brigade establishes two posts close to Regina in the vicinity of the Pys and Miraumont Roads. Some heavy shelling on both sides. At 10.45 p.m. it is reported that enemy aircraft have blown up an ammunition dump near Meaulte. A scouting party from the Right Brigade work down Farmer Road to Dyke Road, patrolling as far as Aqueduct Road and locating some machine-gun emplacements. Other patrols work westward along the whole front. The Germans have thrown out a quantity of new wire.

November 7th.

Heavy bombardment of our line west of Dyke Road while our artillery retaliates on Coulée and Below Trenches. German wire appears very thick and strong along the Below Trench between the Quadrilateral and the Coulée Trench. Enemy busy building new machine-gun emplacements on Grundy Road, and placing wire.

November 8th.

Courcelette shelled heavily during the afternoon. Patrols report a new trench connecting Desire Trench with East Miraumont Road. Arrangements made for attack by 10th and 11th Brigades as soon as weather permitted two days' preliminary bombardment.

November 9th.

It is proposed to capture and consolidate Regina Trench from the 11th Brigade block east of the Pys Road, to Farmer Road and to establish strong blocks at the junctions and beyond, north of Regina Trench. A fine day, and a most successful shoot was carried out upon Regina Trench.

November 10th.

The heavy artillery bombardment of Regina continued and preparations made for the attack. Hostile aircraft attack dumps and depots behind our lines.

November 11th.

At midnight 10th-11th, the 10th and 11th Brigades attack and capture the German portion of Regina Trench to Farmer Road. All objectives gained, though the 102nd Battalion, in the northern attack, unable to maintain a post as far north of Regina as had been hoped. A very successful attack—the positions consolidated by 3 a.m. and later several counter-attacks beaten off. The 12th Brigade relieve the 10th and 11th Brigades in the new line.

November 12th.

The 12th Brigade pushing out advanced trenches to gain observation over the Coulée and Below Trenches. Our heavy guns bombard Desire Support Trench successfully with little hostile shelling in reply. A portion of the trenches on the extreme right taken over by the 48th British Division.

November 13th.

The British Division attack on the Canadian left, and the enemy place a barrage on our right Battalion lines and Dyke Road. Our new salient in Regina Trench heavily shelled. Our patrols busy.

November 14th.

The German artillery very active all day, throwing a quantity of gas shells into our lines. Enemy aircraft raid our camps and bases during the night. Our artillery retaliates on Below Trench and hostile communications.

November 15th.

10th Brigade patrols in touch with the enemy in the southern portion of Below Trench. It is proposed to extend our line in that direction. Enemy shell 10th Brigade front, 10th Street, and Bapaume Road.

Preparations for an offensive on the 18th.

November 16th.

Enemy place a heavy barrage on 10th Brigade sectors, and continue until checked by the retaliation of our artillery. The 11th Brigade takes over the frontage of the 54th Brigade, 18th Division.

Instructions issued for the attack. 10th Brigade to advance their line from the apex of Regina Trench on the right to the junction of the German new trench with Desire Support. The 11th Brigade to take over the front now held by the 54th Brigade, 18th Division and advance their line to the line of the Desire Support Trench as far west as a point in the Ravine, 100 yards east of where the Ravine turns north.

November 17th.

Our artillery bombarding the German line, the new trench north of Regina, the southern portion of Below Trench and the Coulée Trench.

Some successful wire cutting accomplished.

November 18th.

Barrage starts at 6 a.m. and the operations successfully carried out. Our guns succeed in capturing Desire Trench from the Ravine to a point about halfway between the Pys and East Miraumont Roads. East of this point our men have great trouble, meeting with heavy artillery and machine-gun fire, and are ultimately driven back to Regina Trench. Parties from the 38th and 87th Battalions advance into Grandcourt Trench and take many prisoners, but later are ordered to retire and assist in the consolidation of the new line running about 100 yards north of Desire Trench. The operation as a whole distinctly successful, in spite of the reverse on the right.

November 19th.

No sign of hostile artillery retaliation or counter-attack during the day. Our heavy artillery arranges a shoot to start at junction of New Trench and Below Trench westward to Practice Road to the junction of New Trench and Desire Trench—to clear out the Germans who held up the right of our attack on the 18th. In the meantime Coulée Trench is bombarded with excellent results. The 12th Brigade holding the left of the line from the Ravine to the block in Desire Trench about 250 yards west of the Pys Road, the 11th Brigade from the block along the curve south by south-east to Regina Trench, and to the entrance right of the Division position.

November 20th.

The misty weather postpones the artillery action arranged on the 19th. East of Pys Road the enemy attack our working party, capturing several of the men. Our patrols retaliate on hostile posts. Corps Commanders congratulate the Canadians on the success of the 18th.

November 21st.

The Canadians busy placing the line in a strong defensive position. The artillery offensive postponed owing to the proposed relief of our guns, and the general artillery activity less than usual, though a hostile bombardment of the Regina Trench Road Junction caused some damage to our lines. Enemy appears to be working hard upon his defences.

November 22nd.

184th Brigade, 61st Division, takes over the line from the Ravine to the West Miraumont Road, held by the 12th Brigade. Hostile bombardment of our front line, while our artillery retaliates on a trench running from Below to Desire Support Trench. Many aerial combats, and several planes brought down on both sides.

November 23rd.

The Germans shell New Street, but cause little damage.

The heavy artillery have another and more successful bombardment of the new enemy trench between Below and Desire Trenches, and disperse German working parties in Crest Trench, along the Miraumont Road.

November 24th.

4th Brigade relieves the 11th Brigade. Enemy artillery less active during the day. German infantry observed on the Miraumont Road, and badly cut up by our artillery fire. Grevillers Trench and the junction of Coulée and Below Trenches are shelled.

Orders received from the Corps for the relief and move of the 4th Division.

November 25th.

Preparing for relief, 1st, 2nd, and 3rd Canadian Divisional Artillery relieved by the 51st Divisional Artillery, 10th Brigade relieved in the line by the 12th Brigade, who will hold the entire front line until final relief by the 51st Division. Enemy working hard on defences of New Gallwitz Trench, and our artillery disperses a working party in Crest Trench.

November 26th.

Preparations for move completed. An offensive, arranged by the Yukon Machine-gun Battery, to clear out hostile patrols and working parties. The 10th and 11th Brigades commence their move to Canadian Corps area.

November 27th.

The machine-gun action reported to have been very satisfactory. Enemy artillery quiet, though movement of troops is noted. The 51st Division relieves the 4th Division.

November 28th.

The remainder of the 4th Division leaves the Somme area.

The Division joins the Canadian Corps with the 1st Army on the Arras-Lens front.

THE END.

Map of Regina Trench
showing Operations by Progressive Stages on the next page

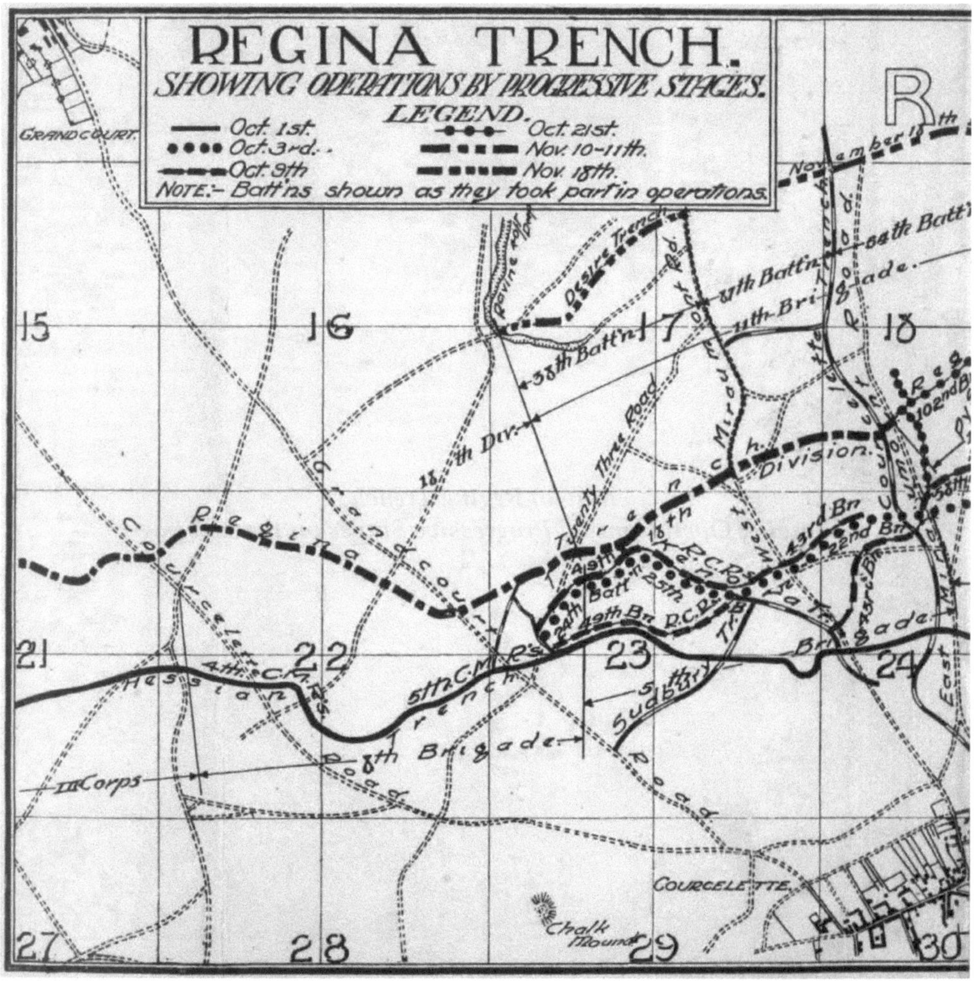

Map—Regina Trench. Showing Operations by Progressive Stages. (Left)

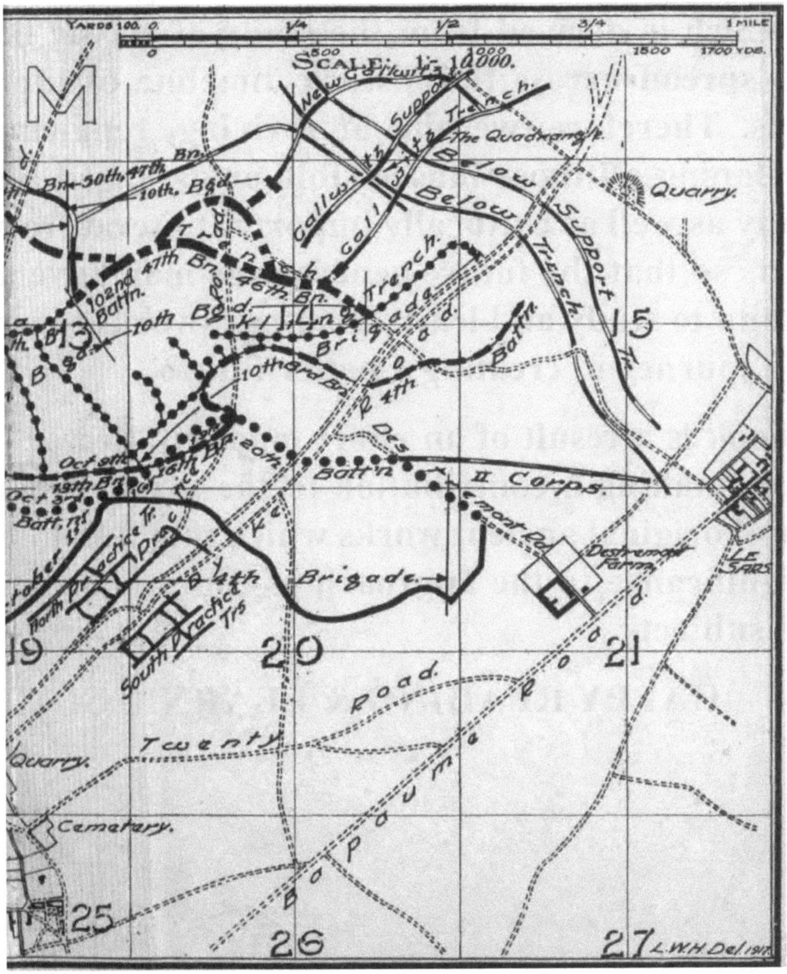

Map—Regina Trench. Showing Operations by Progressive Stages. (Right)

Lector House believes that a society develops through a two-fold approach of continuous learning and adaptation, which is derived from the study of classic literary works spread across the historic timeline of literature records. Therefore, we aim at reviving, repairing and redeveloping all those inaccessible or damaged but historically as well as culturally important literature across subjects so that the future generations may have an opportunity to study and learn from past works to embark upon a journey of creating a better future.

This book is a result of an effort made by Lector House towards making a contribution to the preservation and repair of original ancient works which might hold historical significance to the approach of continuous learning across subjects.

HAPPY READING & LEARNING!

LECTOR HOUSE

LECTOR HOUSE LLP

E-MAIL: info@lectorhouse.com

9 789356 146099

Printed by Libri Plureos GmbH in Hamburg,
Germany

9 789356 146099